22 BT

absolute / relative

DATE			

THE
FOUR DIMENSIONS
OF
PHILOSOPHY

ALSO BY MORTIMER J. ADLER

Dialectic
What Man Has Made of Man
How to Read a Book
A Dialectic of Morals
How to Think About War and Peace
The Revolution in Education (with Milton Mayer)
The Capitalist Manifesto (with Louis O. Kelso)
The Idea of Freedom (2 vols.)
The New Capitalists (with Louis O. Kelso)
The Conditions of Philosophy
The Difference of Man and the Difference It Makes
The Time of Our Lives
The Common Sense of Politics
The American Testament (with William Gorman)
Some Questions About Language
Philosopher at Large
Great Treasury of Western Thought (edited with Charles Van Doren)
Aristotle for Everybody
How to Think About God
Six Great Ideas
The Angels and Us
The Paideia Proposal
How to Speak / How to Listen
Paideia Problems and Possibilities
A Vision of the Future
The Paideia Program (with members of the Paideia Group)
Ten Philosophical Mistakes
A Guidebook to Learning
We Hold These Truths
Reforming Education: The Opening of the American Mind
    (edited by Geraldine Van Doren)
Intellect: Mind Over Matter
Truth in Religion
Haves Without Have-Nots
Desires, Right & Wrong
A Second Look in the Rearview Mirror
The Great Ideas: A Lexicon of Western Thought

THE
FOUR DIMENSIONS
OF
PHILOSOPHY

Metaphysical • Moral • Objective • Categorical

MORTIMER J. ADLER

Macmillan Publishing Company
NEW YORK

Maxwell Macmillan Canada
TORONTO

Maxwell Macmillan International
NEW YORK OXFORD SINGAPORE SYDNEY

Macmillan Publishing Company   Maxwell Macmillan Canada, Inc.
866 Third Avenue   1200 Eglinton Avenue East
New York, NY 10022   Suite 200
   Don Mills, Ontario M3C 3N1

Macmillan Publishing Company is part of the Maxwell
Communication Group of Companies.

Library of Congress Cataloging-in-Publication Data
Adler, Mortimer Jerome, 1902–
    The four dimensions of philosophy: metaphysical, moral,
objective, categorical / Mortimer J. Adler.
      p.   cm.
    Includes index.
    ISBN 0-02-500574-X
    1. Philosophy.   2. Adler, Mortimer Jerome, 1902–.   I. Title.
II. Title: 4 dimensions of philosophy.
B53.A29   1993
101—dc20   92–37758
                                             CIP

10 9 8 7 6 5 4 3 2 1

Designed by Jack Meserole

CONTENTS

Everybody's Business

I

This is a philosophical book about philosophy and about its relation to and difference from other disciplines, such as history, mathematics, and empirical science, and also works of the intellectual imagination, such as stories, novels, and plays. I should add that this Prologue is in part an autobiographical account of my own development in learning what philosophy is and what it is about.

A book about philosophy sometimes is not, strictly speaking, a philosophical book. It may be a historical book, a history of philosophy as a whole or about philosophy at some particular time and place. It may also be a work of scholarly commentary on the contributions of a great philosopher or of a school of philosophical thought, explicating, interpreting, and even criticizing that contribution. In this respect, it is no different from a scholarly commentary on the work of a great scientist.

Both philosophy and history are reflexive in a way that empirical science is not. Not only can there be a history of everything, including all the productions of the human mind—histories of science, of philosophy, of mathematics, of all the arts—but there can also be a history of history itself as an intellectual discipline and as a field of research. So, too, in addition to there being a philosophy of history, of mathemat-

ics, and of science, there can be a philosophical consideration
of philosophy itself, answering such questions as: What is the
scope of the philosophical enterprise? What is its method?
What are the criteria of excellence in philosophical work?
How does philosophy relate to and differ from other intellectual disciplines? and so on.

Unlike history and philosophy, empirical science is not
reflexive. When empirical scientists write about science,
they are not writing as scientists but as historians or philosophers. If scientists were to dispute with me concerning
what I have to say in this book about the limitations of
scientific knowledge or the independence of philosophy
from science, they would have to do so as philosophers, not
as scientists. There is no scientific knowledge or understanding of these matters.

This may come as a shock to many readers who have
adopted the euphoric use of the word "scientific," as if it
were the mark of excellence in all intellectual work. If a piece
of work is scientific, it is good; if it is not scientific, it is
defective in one way or another. To call a historian scientific
is to compliment him, even though there is no such thing as
scientific history any more than there can be scientific philosophy. This aggrandizement of science in the twentieth century is one of the difficulties that in our day the philosophical
enterprise must overcome in order to achieve its proper place
in our culture as a whole, in some respects a place superior to
that of science, in other respects, not so.

One can be a generally educated human being without
being knowledgeable in this or that specialized field of empirical science. Such knowledge belongs to the specialist, not
the generalist. But one cannot be a generally educated human
being without knowing the history of science and without
having some philosophical understanding of science. Becoming a generally educated human being also involves
some grasp of the history of history and of philosophy, and

some understanding of the philosophy of history and of philosophy.

That is one reason I say that philosophy is everybody's business. Everyone is not called upon to be a lawyer, a physician, an accountant, or an engineer; nor for that matter is everyone called upon to engage in some field of historical or scientific research. But everyone is called upon to philosophize; thinking individuals, whether they know it or not, have some traces of philosophical insight or analysis in their moments of reflection. To be reflective about one's experience or about what human beings call their common sense is to be philosophical about it.

Why philosophy is everybody's business, as no other use of one's mind is, will become clearer, I hope, as this book about philosophy develops. Even though this cannot be fully explained at the beginning, the point should be made at the outset, with one initial clarification. To say that every thinking individual is, in reflective moments, a philosopher, and that everyone philosophizes and is enriched by doing so is not to say that everyone should aspire to become a professor of philosophy. For the most part, as the academic world is organized and operated today, almost all professors of philosophy are specialists in some limited area of philosophy, not moving competently in all its four dimensions, especially not in its third and fourth.

2

When I decided at age fifteen that I wanted to make philosophy my lifelong vocation I had read, by sheer accident, only two philosophical books. One was a dialogue by Plato, the *Euthyphro*, through which I became acquainted with the Socratic method of philosophical inquiry—asking questions and pursuing the answers to them by continuing to ask questions elicited by these answers. I was inspired to try to use that method in conversations with my friends. I did not know at that time that being persistently Socratic in dealing with the minds of others was being on the road to becoming a philosopher.

The other book I read at the time was *Pragmatism* by William James—his lectures given at Columbia University in 1908. He had written books on psychology before, but this was his first major effort in philosophy. Its opening chapter contains eloquent passages on how philosophy plays a role in the lives of everyone. It also corrects and dismisses some current mistakes about what philosophy is and is not.

Readers should catch me in an apparent contradiction at this point. On the one hand, I started out by saying that philosophy is everybody's business. Now, on the other hand, I appear to be saying that at the age of fifteen I decided on making philosophy my life's vocation. Not many boys of fifteen do that; nor, for that matter, do most human beings choose philosophy as the vocation to which they devote their lives. They choose to become businessmen, statesmen, lawyers, physicians, engineers, economists, empirical scientists, historians, mathematicians, musicians, architects, dramatists, novelists, and so on.

If only a few human beings choose philosophy as a vocation, instead of all the other vocations just mentioned, how, then, critical readers will ask, can you say that philosophy is everybody's business?

I hope my solution to the problem will not seem like quibbling on my part. I said that philosophy was everybody's *business,* and that every thinking individual philosophizes from time to time in life's most reflective moments. I did not say that everyone was obligated to make philosophy his or her life's *vocation.*

This is like saying that everyone should be concerned with the health of his or her body. To say that is not contradicted by saying that only some human beings choose to become physicians as their life's vocation. Being concerned with the health and vitality of one's own body is an obvious human obligation. Acquiring the vocational skills of medicine in order to become a physician is not a human obligation but the free choice of certain individuals.

Similarly, being concerned with the vitality and perfection of one's own mind is a human obligation. But acquiring the skills of philosophical thought and deciding to make philosophical thought a lifelong vocation is a free choice on the part of a small number of individuals.

A good family physician may rightly rebuke a patient for being negligent in the care of his health or that of his family. In addition, the physician can use his vocational skills to help the patient correct such negligence. Similarly, a person whose vocation is philosophy may exhort others to philosophize for the good of their minds and may help as many as he or she can to do so by giving philosophical lectures or writing philosophical books. The great philosophers are those who have reached and helped a great many people in this way.

The parallelism stops at this point. A good family physician has a limited number of patients that he can help in his medical practice. Philosophers are not limited in this way. Ideally, mankind is the audience at which they aim when they try to disseminate the philosophical insights and wisdom they have acquired in the course of practicing their vocation. The great philosophers are the few who have been most successful in this effort.

3

Since 1928, I have written many philosophical books on a wide variety of subjects. I have written many other books that are philosophical only in part. In addition, I have written many essays and one two-volume work (*The Idea of Freedom*)[1] that are dialectical rather than philosophical. These writings were conceived as being in the service of philosophy. How dialectical work differs from philosophical thought and how it benefits philosophy I will try to explain later.

In the sixty years that have elapsed since I wrote *Dialectic*[2] in 1927, I have written only one book about philosophy itself. Based on the Britannica lectures that I delivered at the University of Chicago in 1964, this book was published in 1965 under the title *The Conditions of Philosophy*.[3] It was addressed to anyone troubled, as I am, by the present state of philosophy, and concerned with its place in liberal education, in our universities, and in our culture.

John Dewey, in his last public appearance before the students at Columbia University, "gave it as his parting message," Professor John Randall reports, "that the most important question in philosophy today is, 'What is philosophy itself? What is the nature and function of the philosophical enterprise?'" The consideration of these questions leads to questions about the relation of philosophy to other disciplines, especially science, mathematics, and religion; and also to questions about the past and future of the philosophical enterprise as well as about its condition today. Such questions spell out the query that people raise when the subject of philosophy is broached: What is it about? What is it up to?

This book attempts to answer these questions in a way that makes sense toward the end of the twentieth century. The answers here proposed have been maturing in my mind since I began the study of philosophy at Columbia more than

[1] *The Idea of Freedom*, 2 vols. (Garden City, N.Y.: Doubleday, Vol. I, 1958; Vol. II, 1961).
[2] *Dialectic* (London: Kegan Paul, Trench Trubner, and New York: Harcourt, Brace, 1927).
[3] *The Conditions of Philosophy: Its Checkered Past, Its Present Disorder, and Its Future Promise* (New York: Atheneum, 1965).

seventy years ago. At various times in my intellectual career I have answered them in ways that no longer seem tenable to me. It would be presumptuous to say that the answers at which I have now arrived (through the correction of earlier errors and the amendment of earlier formulations) are the final answers, but I am persuaded that they come much closer to being the right answers than any which I have hitherto entertained.

The title of the 1965 book used the word "conditions" in two senses. On the one hand, it expressed concern about the present condition of philosophy, especially in the period since the end of the Second World War. On the other hand, it meant that this book was concerned with the conditions to be met if philosophy were ever to improve its present condition.

I mentioned at the outset of this prologue that *Pragmatism* by William James occasioned my decision to become a philosopher. At the same time, it also discouraged me by leading me to become aware of certain views of philosophy that demean it by unfavorable comparison with empirical science, mathematics, and historical research.

One such view was that philosophy dealt with persistent problems, persistent because no solution to them could be agreed upon by those deemed competent to judge. Another was that philosophy was engaged with problems that science had not yet been able to solve, and that when science succeeded in solving them, philosophy would move into the penumbra on the edge of advancing science, to problems that would remain philosophical problems only until science, advancing further, solved them.

In mathematics and in historical research, as well as in empirical science, there is controversy among competing hypotheses and theories, but in all these fields controversies get resolved, agreement replaces disagreement, and progress is made. In comparison to these other fields of intellectual work, philosophy seems to be the field of unresolved controversy, in which agreements do not replace disagreements, and little or no progress is made.

The comparison of philosophy with these other fields of intellectual work disturbed me by making me feel that philosophy was not as respectable a vocation as these others or simply not respectable at all. Why should one spend one's life engaged in controversies that cannot be resolved, with no hope of getting generally agreed upon solutions, with no hope of making progress?

"Respectability" may seem like a strange word to use for what philosophy lacks in our culture today. To understand its connotation, one only need recall the place that philosophy occupied in antiquity, in the Middle Ages, and until very recently even in modern times.

In Greek antiquity and in the Hellenistic period of the ancient Roman world, philosophy was supreme among the intellectual vocations. Philosophical contemplation was for Plato and Aristotle the highest good to be attained in this life. Philosophy was the name for the pursuit of truth about the most fundamental things to be known and understood. As the etymology of the word itself proclaimed, philosophy is the love of wisdom, the most desirable of all the goods of the mind. The Greek word *epistēmē* and its Latin equivalent, *scientia*, named aspects of the philosophical enterprise, not an enterprise that is quite distinct and separate from philosophy, as the empirical sciences are today.

In the Middle Ages, theology was the queen of the sciences and philosophy was her handmaiden. In that era, except for sacred theology, all the branches of knowledge that were independent of religious faith were called sciences and were regarded as branches of philosophy. Even in early modern times, in the seventeenth and eighteenth centuries, the emerging empirical scientists, such as Galileo, Newton, and Gilbert, referred to themselves as philosophers. Isaac Newton's classic on celestial and terrestrial mechanics bore the title *Mathematical Principles of Natural Philosophy*. Not until the late eighteenth century and the present era was philosophy dethroned and replaced by the empirical natural sciences at the pinnacle of culture.

Positivism may have its roots in the skepticism of David Hume,[4] but not until Auguste Comte in the nineteenth century and until this century is it, paradoxically, a philosophical movement that holds the empirical sciences to be the only valid knowledge of reality and thought of the first order. Metaphysics and ethics, which once were the architectonic branches of theoretical and practical philosophy, are not only demeaned, but also removed from the sphere of valued knowledge and relegated to the sphere of personal prejudices and unfounded opinions. The philosophical work of the positivists is work of the second order, serving merely to clarify and organize the achievements of the empirical sciences.

What has come to be called analytical and linguistic philosophy is the other widely prevalent trend in Anglo-American philosophy in this century. It, too, is philosophical work of the second order, being concerned with thought itself and its expression in language, instead of with physical nature, human society, and human affairs, as the empirical sciences are.

I hope I have made clear why, when I wrote *The Conditions of Philosophy* in 1964, I asked myself under what conditions philosophy could regain the respectability and the self-respect it had in past cultural epochs, before the empirical sciences became culturally dominant as they are today. I would like to see philosophy as estimable as it once was, or

---

[4]"If we take in our hand any volume; of divinity or school metaphysics . . . let us ask, *Does it contain any abstract reasoning concerning quantity or number?* No. *Does it contain any experimental reasoning concerning matter of fact and existence?* No. Commit it then to the flames: for it can contain nothing but sophistry and illusion" (David Hume, *An Enquiry Concerning Human Understanding*, Section XII, Part III).

at least as generally esteemed as science for the contributions it makes to our culture and to our lives.

I do not mean to say that philosophy did not have its detractors in prior ages, but only that philosophers in ancient and mediaeval times never asked themselves whether philosophy was worthy of respect. Plato defended philosophy against the sophists and businessmen of his day. Scholastic philosophers defended it against contempt for the vanity of all worldly learning and against a certain type of dogmatic theologian who treated philosophy as theology's handmaiden in a wholly servile sense of that term. But prior to the seventeenth century, philosophers themselves never doubted the respectability of their calling and its role or value in education and in society. There is not the slightest evidence of such concern to be found in their writings.

That concern begins in the seventeenth century. Starting with Descartes, most of the eminent figures in modern philosophy manifest worry about the state of philosophy, its achievements, its progress, its relation to other disciplines. The evidence of this concern is their intense preoccupation with new methods, new organons, new points of departure for philosophy; or their therapeutic recommendations, reforms, reconstructions to cure whatever it is they think is ailing philosophy and to improve its condition.

We find such manifestations in Leibniz and Spinoza as well as in Descartes, Francis Bacon, Thomas Hobbes, and most poignantly in that extraordinary triumvirate—Locke, Berkeley, and Hume—who are responsible with Descartes for most of what has happened and is still happening in philosophy. In consequence, we have the Kantian attempt to lay down a new ground plan with safe and secure foundations for all valid knowledge; and this is followed in the nineteenth century by the various post-Kantian constructions that override Kant's cautions and transgress his critical restrictions on the philosophical enterprise.

Finally, in reaction to these excesses the pendulum swings back in the twentieth century, and we have all the varieties of philosophical reformation, reconstruction, new departures, and therapeutic programs that are associated with American pragmatism, logical positivism (both Viennese and British), analytic and linguistic philosophy (both British and American), and phenomenology and existentialism (mainly European).

If there is any one thing that all these philosophical movements have in common, it is their anxiety about the blind alleys into which philosophy has stumbled, their concern with its validity and its significance, and their effort to remedy its condition and set it off on a new path toward prosperity and progress.

There is, perhaps, one other thing that modern considerations of philosophy's condition have in common. The modern thinkers who ask themselves, in effect, whether philosophy is quite respectable or how to make it so do not themselves hold philosophy prior to the seventeenth century in high esteem.

We are thus confronted with the fact that the earlier philosophers, who never doubted the intellectual respectability of what they were engaged in, do not have the respect of modern and contemporary thinkers, least of all from those who are most concerned about the respectability of philosophy itself.

Among my readers there may be those who would be willing to stop right here. *The problem of philosophy's intellectual respectability does not interest them.* I want to ask such readers to perform an intellectual experiment, which may open their minds to the importance of the problems dealt with in the remaining chapters of this book.

Try to imagine a world in which everything else is exactly the same, but from which philosophy is totally absent. I do not mean just academic philosophy; I mean philosophizing in every degree—that done almost unconsciously by ordinary men and women or inexpertly by scientists, historian, poets, and novelists, as well as that done with technical competence by professional philosophers.

Since philosophizing is an ingrained and inveterate human tendency, I know that it is hard to imagine a world without philosophy in which everything else is the same, including human nature; yet it is certainly no harder than imagining a world without sex as one in which everything else is the same.

In the world I have asked you to imagine, all the other arts and sciences remain continuing enterprises; history and science are taught in colleges and universities; and it is assumed without question that everyone's education should include some acquaintance with them. But philosophy is completely expunged. No one asks any philosophical questions; no one philosophizes; no one has any philosophical knowledge, insight, or understanding; philosophy is not taught or learned; and no philosophical books exist.

Would this make any difference to you? Would you be completely satisfied to live in such a world? Or would you come to the conclusion that it lacked something of importance?

You would realize—would you not?—that even though education involved acquiring historical and scientific knowledge, it could not include any understanding of either science or history, since questions about history and science (other than questions of fact) are not historical or scientific but philosophical questions. You would also realize that a great many of your opinions or beliefs, shared with most of your fellowmen, would have to go unquestioned, because to question them would be to philosophize; they would remain unenlightened opinions or beliefs, because any enlightenment on these matters would have to come from philosophizing about them. You would be debarred from asking questions about yourself and your life, questions about the shape of the world and your place in it, questions about what you should be doing and what you should be seeking—all questions that, in one form or another, you do, in fact, often ask and would find it difficult to desist from asking.

This experiment does not solve the problems with which this book is concerned. It merely justifies the effort, by writer and reader, of considering the conditions that academic or technical philosophy must satisfy in order to provide the guidance it should give to everyone in his efforts to philosophize; and in order to supply the enlightenment that we know, or should know, to be unobtainable from history and science and that, therefore, would be lacking in a world bereft of philosophy.

4

Some works of the mind are productions that individuals undertake and complete by themselves. They are singularly private enterprises, unlike the public enterprises in which many individuals interact and cooperate to produce the desired result. Examples of such private enterprises are to be found in all the arts, the useful as well as the fine arts, especially the latter. Whether the plays of Shakespeare were written by him or by the Earl of Oxford, we can be relatively sure that they were the work of a single individual, not a collaborative effort of many. The same can be said of most of the great paintings that we admire and of the great musical compositions.

Let me use the word "poetry" not just for all imaginative literature—its epic and dramatic poetry as well as its lyrics—but extend it to cover all works of fine art. The Greek word *poiesis,* from which it is derived, warrants that extension, for it means "making" as opposed to *praxis,* which means "doing" or "acting."

Two things are to be said about all the works of poetry. First, as already stated, all or most of them are private enterprises. Second, the kind of truth they have—poetical truth—is not exclusionary. Many stories have been told about the same themes—for example, the three Greek tragedies about Electra and Orestes, the children of Agamemnon and Clytemnestra. The Renaissance paintings of Madonna and child furnish another example of the nonexclusionary character of poetical treatments of the same subject. One is not true and all the others false; they all are permissable treatments of the subject, having varying degrees of verisimilitude and of insight.

But when we pass from poetry to science, we pass from the realm of poetical truth to the realm of factual and logical truth, and this mode of truth is exclusionary. If there are conflicting scientific hypotheses or theories, they cannot all be true. If one is true, the others with which it is logically incompatible must be false.

Another difference between poetry and the empirical sciences is that the latter, especially as developed in this century, are public and cooperative enterprises. Many individuals interact and work together to produce this century's extraordinary achievements in scientific research and its technological applications. Without such interaction and cooperation that characterizes science as a public enterprise, the advances we applaud might not have occurred.

In the early centuries of modern times, the philosophical enterprise often appears to resemble poetry more than it does science. The reason that is so stems from the fact that in the sixteenth and seventeenth centuries, eminent philosophers, such as Descartes, Hobbes, Spinoza, and Leibniz—and in later centuries, German philosophers such as Kant, Hegel, and Schopenhauer—constructed systems of thought. Philosophical systems differ from one another as poetical works do. They do not argue with one another. They are differing world pictures or world views rather than being like conflicting hypotheses or theories, the contradictions or incompatibilities between which can be resolved.

Philosophical systems are a peculiarly modern—and regrettable—phenomenon. We do not find them in the dialogues of Plato or in the treatises of Aristotle; nor can we find a trace of them in the great philosophical works of the Middle Ages.

Aristotle's procedure in the opening pages of most of his treatises is to survey what his predecessors or contemporaries have to say on the subject with which he is dealing, and then to try to sift the wheat from the chaff. It is worth quoting here two passages in which he explicitly summarizes this procedure in philosophical work as a public and cooperative enterprise.

In Book II, Chapter 1 of his *Metaphysics,* he writes:

> The investigation of the truth is in one way hard, in another easy. An indication of this is found in the fact that no one is able to attain the truth adequately, while, on the other hand, we do not collectively fail, but every one says something true about the nature of things, and while individually we contribute little or nothing to the truth, by the union of all a considerable amount is amassed.

In Book I, Chapter 2 of his treatise *On the Soul,* Aristotle writes:

> . . . it is necessary . . . to call into council the views of those of our predecessors . . . in order that we may profit by whatever is sound in their suggestions and avoid their errors.

5

Before I wrote *The Conditions of Philosophy* in 1964, I had been prepared to do so by a number of things, all of which had contributing influences on me. Let me enumerate them briefly.

(1) One was an essay by Professor Arthur O. Lovejoy of Johns Hopkins University—his presidential address at the

meeting of the American Philosophical Association in 1916, entitled "On Some Conditions of Progress in Philosophical Inquiry."[5] I read this when I was a young instructor at Columbia University, greatly perplexed by the lack of agreement among philosophers and the absence of progress in their field of work.

In this essay Professor Lovejoy remarks that "dialogue, discussion, and the interaction of two or more minds is the very essence of the method" by which philosophy could hope to make progress. The method described I later called the dialectical method that could be employed to determine precisely the objects about which philosophers disagreed and about which they should join issue. Such interactive and cooperative work on their part would clarify the great controversies that are to be found in the history of philosophy.

I had Professor Lovejoy's essay in mind when I wrote *Dialectic* in 1927 and projected a dialectical undertaking on the part of philosophers that would enable them to make progress in the pursuit of truth. This should occur before they engaged in argument with one another about their doctrinal disagreements. They could at least agree dialectically, if not doctrinally; that is, they could agree about the issues that confronted them.

But it was not until 1952 that I was enabled by a large grant from the Ford Foundation to establish an institute to initiate such dialectical work as propaedeutic to progress in philosophy. In the first annual report of the Institute's work, I cited Professor Lovejoy's essay as my inspiration and guidance in planning the work of the Institute.[6]

---

[5]This was published in *The Philosophical Review*, Vol. XXVI, No. 2, March 1917, pp. 123–63.

[6] I misnamed the institute by calling it the Institute for Philosophical Research. It should have been called the Institute for Dialectical Research. That would have been quite accurate, as the other title that the Institute has borne all these years is not.

The first work undertaken by a large staff of researchers over a period of eight years resulted in my being able to write the two volumes of *The Idea of Freedom,* the first published in 1958 and the second in 1961. In subsequent years, other members of the Institute's staff wrote dialectical clarifications of the controversies with respect to progress, justice, love, happiness, and religion.

This is not the place to summarize the method we employed in doing this work or the stages in the process of doing it. But I must report that one of our principal findings, in the case of freedom, completely confirmed Professor Lovejoy's suspicion about the serious defects in philosophical controversies. We found that, in the age-old controversy about freedom of choice, the voluminous literature on which extended from antiquity to the present day, adherents of causal determinism who denied that human beings had freedom of choice did not join issue with those who asserted that human beings are natively endowed with a will that has the power of free choice. Their arguments against one another misfired and passed by each other like ships in the night.[7]

In the middle 1940s, I wrote essays on the 102 ideas that went into the *Syntopicon* that was attached to *Great Books of the Western World,* published in 1952.[8] I did not then realize that these essays were a kind of dialectical summation of Western thought on basic philosophical controversies that had been poorly carried on because the philosophers so seldom joined issue and argued relevantly against one another. Though I wrote all of the 102 essays, that could not have been done by me without the help of the large staff of readers that were engaged in producing the *Syntopicon.*

---

[7] I have explained this in Chapter 7 of *Ten Philosophical Mistakes* (New York: Macmillan, 1985), in which I showed why the arguments of the determinists against freedom of choice have persistently missed the point.

[8] These 102 essays have recently been published by Macmillan in a separate volume under the title *The Great Ideas: A Lexicon of Western Thought* (1992).

I was thoroughly conscious, however, of the difference
between the kind of writing that reports the findings of dialectical research and the kind of writing that expounds an
individual's own philosophical views. Since this difference is
so important to the understanding of philosophy itself, let me
state it briefly here.

Dialectical writing abstains from making judgments about
the truth or falsity of the philosophical views or doctrines it
surveys. To proceed dialectically, one must deal with all the
differing views one encounters with complete impartiality and
neutrality—that is, without favoring one point of view
against another. One must be point of viewless in treating all
points of view.

To be a philosopher, one must make up one's own mind
about where the truth lies on the great issues that have filled
the pages of philosophical controversy.[9] Some of the same
ideas that I wrote about dialectically in the *Syntopicon* essays
I have more recently written philosophical essays about. In
these I argued for the truth of the views I then espoused,
against the opposing view that I rejected as erroneous.[10]

(2) A second preparatory influence was my reading of
Jacques Maritain's *An Introduction to Philosophy* in the
1930s.[11] Instead of quoting the passages that I found so enlightening, let me distill from memory the controlling insights
that I took away from reading that book.[12]

---

[9]It would be helpful to a philosopher who tried to separate the truth from the
manifold errors that surround it if philosophical controversy had been carried on
well.

[10]See *Six Great Ideas* (New York: Macmillan, 1981).

[11]Jacques Maritain, *An Introduction to Philosophy,* trans. from the eleventh
French edition by E. I. Watkin (London: Sheed & Ward, 1930).

[12]See Ibid., pp. 44–45, 61–63, 76–77, 102–103, and especially Chapter VII, pp.
135, 137, 141–43. My memory of these insights goes beyond what is to be found in
the book, for it was enriched by lectures that Maritain gave at the University of
Chicago in the 1930s and by the many conversations we had after we became close
friends.

Here are the four points that influenced me:

—Only in ancient Greece was philosophy distinct and separate from the religious beliefs and practices of the local culture, and totally unaffected by them.
—In relation to modern empirical science, philosophy is autonomous in the sense that its principles and conclusions are not in any way dependent on the current state of or the advances in the empirical sciences.
—Philosophy has a method of its own that enables it to answer questions that cannot be answered by the method of the empirical sciences, of historical research, or of mathematics.
—While it corrects and refines some of the opinions and convictions held by common sense, philosophy is nevertheless continuous with common sense and elucidates its deepest convictions by providing their rational basis and elaboration.

This last point throws light on why philosophy is everybody's business. Common sense is a common human possession. We all live in the same world, participate in common elements in our experience of it, having human minds that are specifically the same in all members of the species. Hence, when human beings philosophize in moments of reflection about the serious problems that confront everyone, they have the same background for doing so. Only those who make philosophy their lifelong vocation acquire the intellectual skills to go deeper and further than reflective individuals who have common sense.

(3) The third preparatory influence consisted of two lectures that I delivered in the years before I wrote *The Conditions of Philosophy*. Both manifested the influence of Maritain. One was entitled "The Questions Science Cannot Answer," questions that, in my judgment, were more im-

portant than any of the questions that science can answer.[13]

The other lecture was entitled "Modern Science and Ancient Wisdom." It recognized that, with very few exceptions, philosophy had suffered a very serious decline in modern times, the same era when, simultaneously, the empirical sciences had risen to cultural dominance.[14]

(4) Finally, the last preparatory step occurred in the 1950s after Jacques Maritain had become associated with the Institute for Philosophical Research and had contributed to the formulations that went into the writing of *The Idea of Freedom*. He not only participated in the dialectical work of the Institute; he was also acquainted with the dialectical essays on the 102 great ideas that I had written for the *Syntopicon*.

Though Maritain expressed unqualified admiration of the essays in the *Syntopicon* and of *The Idea of Freedom*, he said to me that he thought I had spent enough of my time and energy doing dialectical work, and that from now on I should engage in philosophical thought and, to the best of my ability, in the pursuit of philosophical truth.

I took the advice seriously, as is attested by most of the books I have written since the middle 1960s. The first of these books, *The Conditions of Philosophy*, was my attempt to get at the truth about philosophy itself, about which at the time there were so many differences of opinion, if not clear and precise disagreements.

---

[13] I concentrated on the difference between scientific and philosophical problems, first, because in our day it is the relation of philosophy to the empirical sciences that is of critical importance; and, second, because it is obvious that philosophy can answer questions that cannot be answered by historical research or mathematical thought.

[14] The gist of this lecture became the Epilogue in *Ten Philosophical Mistakes*, a book dealing with philosophical errors that have occurred only in modern times.

6

Part One of this book is a recapitulation of the main theses and insights to be found in *The Conditions of Philosophy*. That book has been out of print for many years and is not easily accessible. The main points in it constitute the background of the present book and must be expounded briefly as the basis for going further. I hope to do that in Part One, either by summary restatements of its message or by quoting passages from it.

From the philosophical work that I have done in the years since I wrote *The Conditions of Philosophy*, I have learned more about the variety of tasks that philosophy performs than I clearly perceived at the earlier date. At that time I concentrated mainly on the first two dimensions of philosophy, in which philosophy is a mode of both theoretical and practical knowledge (i.e., metaphysical and moral knowledge) quite distinct from the knowledge gained by empirical science, historical research, and mathematical thought. These two aspects of the philosophical enterprise will be covered in the chapters of Part Two.

I now realize that the achievements of philosophy go beyond metaphysical and moral knowledge. The other two dimensions of philosophy lie in the sphere of understanding rather than knowledge—the understanding of ideas as objects of thought and the understanding of all the special disciplines that represent the departments of intellectual work. These two dimensions will be covered in Part Three.

This book will conclude with an Epilogue concerned with the future of philosophy and the role of dialectical efforts to assure greater progress than philosophy has achieved in the past.

PART ONE

The Conditions

of Philosophy:

A Recapitulation

CHAPTER 1

An Autonomous Branch

of Knowledge

I

In *The Conditions of Philosophy,* I set forth six conditions that philosophy would have to satisfy in order to regain its rightful place in contemporary culture, in our academic institutions, and in the esteem of the general public, not to mention the self-respect individuals should enjoy in making philosophy their life's vocation. The six conditions were:

(i) that philosophy should be recognized as an autonomous branch of knowledge;

(ii) that philosophical knowledge should be like the knowledge attained in the natural sciences; that is, it should be knowledge of the first order, knowledge of the reality of the world of physical nature and not merely knowledge of the second order;

(iii) that philosophical theories and conclusions should be judged by the same standard of objective truth that applies to the empirical natural sciences;

(iv) that philosophy could be conducted as a public, not a private enterprise, through the interaction and cooperation of many who are at work in its sphere of inquiry;

(v) that philosophy as a mode of inquiry should have a method distinctively its own, by which it can answer questions that cannot be answered by the methods of other modes of inquiry;

(vi) that philosophy should not be esoteric, that is, out of touch with the world of ordinary human beings and with the commonsense opinions they hold.

In this and succeeding chapters, I will attempt to explicate and elaborate these six points, beginning in this chapter with the first of these.

2

The three critical words in the statement of the first condition are "autonomous," "branch," and "knowledge." The word "branch" tells us that philosophy is only one branch of knowledge and that there are other branches of knowledge to which philosophy may stand in some relation. Hence its autonomy may not be one of complete independence; it may have only limited autonomy. Before I explain how its autonomy is limited, let me address myself to the most troublesome of the three words—"knowledge."

In the history of Western thought, the word "knowledge" is used in two senses, one of which states an ideal that is not realized in any of the recognized branches of knowledge—not in the empirical sciences, not in history, and not even in mathematics. If that is the case, then philosophy should not be expected to be knowledge in that ideal sense.

In this idealized sense, knowledge consists of truths known beyond the shadow of a doubt, incorrigible and immutable truths involving self-evident propositions and conclusions that can be validly deduced from them.

The Greek word for knowledge in this idealized sense was *epistēmē*; in the Roman world its Latin equivalent was *scien-*

tia. For many centuries, mathematical systems were thought to exemplify the ideal of incorrigible knowledge with certitude; and philosophers, such as Descartes and Spinoza, tried to set forth their doctrines in a style that imitated mathematics.

The rise of epistemology in modern times represents the effort of more skeptical philosophers to challenge this pretension to certitude in philosophical thought. We now know, through the work of Kurt Gödel in the early part of this century, that even a consistent, axiomatic mathematical system contains propositions that may be true, but the truth of which is formally undecidable.

If we do not claim for mathematics, empirical science, or philosophy that these disciplines attain incorrigible truth, in what sense of "knowledge," then, are we speaking when we claim for philosophy that it is a branch of knowledge?

If it does not consist in knowing incorrigible truths, truths beyond the shadow of a doubt, it may still be knowledge though it remains in the realm of doubt, for its truths are subject to correction and amendment when new evidence is discovered or new reasons are advanced.

The judgments made about such truths may be beyond a reasonable doubt or they may be supported by only a preponderance of evidence in their favor, but so long as they remain in the realm of doubt they also remain subject to further correction or amendment. They never become incorrigible; our judgments about them never attain finality and certitude.[1]

If it is in this sense of the word that empirical science can claim to be knowledge, then when we claim that philosophy is a branch of knowledge we should be satisfied to use the

---

[1] The truth or falsity of propositions that are entertained with suspended judgment is immutable. What changes from time to time is the correctness of our judgments about the truth of propositions. When we affirm a proposition that, as entertained, is true, our judgment is correct. It is our judgments that are corrigible and amendable as our knowledge grows and improves.

word in the same sense. The Greeks had a word for knowledge in this more moderate sense. For them it was *doxa*, contrasted with *epistēmē*, as we in English often use the word "opinion."[2]

Unfortunately, we also use the word "opinion" in the sense that denies it is knowledge at all, even in a moderate sense of the word. In that sense we are speaking of totally unfounded personal opinions, the truth of which is not tested and often is not even testable.

The English philosopher of science Sir Karl Popper makes use of the word *doxa* in drawing the line between what he regards as testable and corrigible knowledge and unfounded opinion. The mark of the latter is that it is not testable and not falsifiable. I regret to add that Professor Popper places philosophy on the side of his dividing line with unfounded, untestable, and unfalsifiable opinion, not with the empirical sciences as testable, falsifiable, and corrigible *doxa*.

Let me summarize this briefly in the following three statements. (1) In the idealized sense of knowledge as *epistēmē*, there is no mode of human inquiry that results in knowledge. (2) In the more moderate sense of knowledge as *doxa* (which is well-founded opinion, based on evidence and reason, opinion that is testable, falsifiable, and corrigible), historical research, mathematical reasoning, empirical science, and philosophy are all branches of knowledge, each with a distinct method or mode of inquiry. (3) In contradistinction to knowledge, both in its idealized sense as *epistēmē* and its more moderate sense of *doxa*, there are totally unfounded opinions—personal prejudices that are untestable.

---

[2] The Greek word *doxa* is found in the English word "orthodoxy," meaning "right doctrine or right opinion." Opinions can be either true or false, right or wrong judgments of the mind, whereas the word "knowledge" always has the connotation of truth possessed by the mind. The phrase "false knowledge" is a contradiction in terms; what is correctly judged by the mind to be false is not knowledge.

3

In what does the limited autonomy of philosophy as a branch of knowledge consist? The method of philosophy as a distinct mode of inquiry enables it to answer questions that are not answerable by any other mode of human inquiry—not by historical research, not by mathematical thought, not by empirical science. In other words, there are *purely* philosophical questions, questions that, to whatever extent they are answerable, are answerable by philosophy alone.

Before I describe the distinctive method of philosophy and contrast it with the methods of other modes of inquiry, let me first formalize this point about the autonomy of distinct branches of knowledge. Let Alpha and Beta stand for branches of knowledge attainable by distinct modes of inquiry. In all modes of human inquiry sense-experience and rational thought play a role, but that role differs from one mode of inquiry to another. If Alpha and Beta are distinct modes of inquiry in which sense-experience and reasoning play some role, then Alpha will be able to answer questions that Beta cannot answer; and conversely, Beta will be able to answer questions that Alpha cannot answer.

Furthermore, the answers that Alpha gives to questions that are answerable by its method cannot be refuted or rejected by Beta employing the method that is distinctive of its mode of inquiry. Thus considered, Alpha and Beta can be said to have limited autonomy. Each is independent of the other with regard to the questions that are proper to its field of inquiry.

This can now be made concretely clear by stating the lines of demarcation which separate the four main branches of knowledge—historical research, empirical science, mathematical thought, and philosophy. A fifth branch, here omitted, is scholarly research in the field of humanities. The reason for its omission is that whatever applies to historical research also applies to it.

CHAPTER 2

Diverse Modes
of Inquiry

I

From the point of view of distinguishing philosophy from empirical science and historical research, the most important criterion is whether the method of these modes of inquiry is investigative or not.

A method is noninvestigative if the branch of knowledge that it serves to develop can be exercised without leaving an armchair and a desk with instruments of writing on it. Mathematical thought is a prime example of noninvestigative or armchair thinking. There is nothing in the world of sense-experience that a mathematician needs to explore by going forth to investigate that world perceptually.

Mathematical or purely theoretical physics is like pure mathematics in this respect, but the empirical science of physics involves experimentation. Knowledge of the physical world grows only when, among the various theoretical formulations developed in mathematical physics, investigative efforts yield decisive empirical data that select the theory or formulation that best fits the facts empirically known at the time.

What has just been said about empirical physical science

as an investigative mode of inquiry applies with minor differences to all the natural sciences, the social sciences, and historical research. This leaves philosophy paired with mathematical thought as a mode of inquiry that can be called armchair thinking because it is noninvestigative.

However, though it is thus paired with mathematics, philosophy as a branch of knowledge (in the moderate sense of that term) is empirically testable and falsifiable as mathematics is not. What may at first appear to be paradoxical in this statement is removed by two further distinctions.

The first is the distinction between synthetic and analytic judgments. A synthetic judgment is testable and falsifiable by sense-experience. By contrast, an analytic judgment is one that can be tested and falsified only by rational processes. That is why mathematics, associated with formal logic, is called a formal rather than an empirical branch of knowledge.

Insofar as philosophy is a branch of knowledge that is concerned with the reality of the world of nature and of human affairs, as well as with other realities that are transempirical, philosophical judgments are synthetic rather than analytical or purely formal. In this respect, it would appear to be associated with the empirical sciences and with historical research rather than with mathematical thought.

To understand how this can be so, we must turn to the second distinction—that between special and common experience. Special experience consists of the data discovered by investigation in the empirical sciences and in historical research. Investigation is always motivated by explicit questions that can be answered by experimentation or by collecting empirical data in other ways. By contrast, common experience is the experience all human beings have in their waking hours, experience that does not occur in answer to specific questions but only as the result of being conscious. We may not even take note of it at the time.

Experience may vary for individuals living in different environments at different times and places, but a core of such experiences is the same for all human beings at all times and places. The negative aspect of common experience is that it consists of all the experience we have *without* asking a single question that calls for steps of observation specially contrived for the purpose. The positive aspect of common experience is that at its core it *includes* experiences that are the same for all human beings at all times and places.

The ordinary day-to-day experiences of a twentieth-century Eskimo, New Yorker, and Hottentot are not the same in all respects. This must also be said of an Athenian of the fourth century B.C., a Parisian of the thirteenth century, and a Bostonian of the twentieth century. But the ordinary day-to-day experiences of these individuals do not differ in all respects. They would be immediately able to communicate with one another about a certain number of things if they were to meet and had a common language for conversation—such things as changes in the seasons, the shift from day to night, living and dying, eating and sleeping, losing and finding, giving and getting, being at rest and moving about in space, and so on. I think we can define this common core human experience that does not result from methodical investigation as comprising those things about which communication is *universally possible* and with regard to which it is possible to translate certain statements made in any human language into equivalent statements in any other.

Let me sum this up by saying that philosophy, like science and history, and unlike mathematics, is empirical, not formal, differing in the character of the experience it uses and relies upon. But it is also like mathematics, and unlike science and history, in being an armchair, or noninvestigative mode of inquiry by virtue of the fact that the experience it uses and upon which it relies is the common core of experience that all human beings have when they are awake and are exercising their senses, but not observing, for the purpose of answering specific questions, the kinds of questions that motivate investigators.

2

It may be helpful to readers trying to understand the distinction between special and common experience if I quote and comment on statements by two twentieth-century philosophers who have, in somewhat different terms, acknowledged the relevance of this distinction in defining philosophy as a distinct mode of inquiry and branch of knowledge.

The first is by Professor A. J. Ayer of Oxford University, in the book *The Problem of Knowledge*. It should be read in light of the view, held by him and other British writers in the group called analytical and linguistic philosophers, that philosophy does not discover new facts about the world and does not test its conclusions by appealing to the data of special observation. Professor Ayer writes:

> Philosophical theories are not tested by observation. They are neutral with respect to particular matters of fact. That is not to say that philosophers are not concerned with facts, but they are in a strange position that all the evidence which bears upon their problems is already available to them.[1]

Must we not ask Professor Ayer: What evidence is available to philosophers without investigation, without special observation, on their part? What is this evidence if it is not to be found in common experience? If there were no such thing as common experience, would philosophers be in the strange position of having all the evidence they need already available to them, where "already available" must mean

---

[1] A. J. Ayer, *The Problem of Knowledge* (London: Macmillan and New York: St. Martin's Press, 1956), p. 1.

"without special efforts of investigation on their part"? The only thing that is "strange" about the position of the philosopher is that, in this respect, he is unlike the scientist who does not have all the evidence he needs already available to him, but must investigate in order to obtain it. To call this "strange" reveals the prevalent modern propensity to regard the procedure of the scientist as standard and normal, and whatever differs from it as odd and somehow abnormal.

The second statement that I think readers will find enlightening is by Professor George Santayana of Harvard University, in his book *Skepticism and Animal Faith*. It throws light on the things that constitute the common core of everyday human experience—the same for all men everywhere at all times because they are all sufficiently the same and because they live in a world that is sufficiently the same. Professor Santayana writes:

> For good or ill, I am an ignorant man, almost a poet, and I can only spread a feast of what everybody knows. Fortunately, exact science and the books of the learned are not necessary to establish my essential doctrine, nor can any of them claim a higher warrant than it has in itself: for it rests on public experience. It needs, to prove it, only the stars, the seasons, the swarm of animals, the spectacle of birth and death, of cities and wars. My philosophy is justified, and has been justified in all ages and countries, by the facts before every man's eyes. . . . In the past or in the future, my language and my borrowed knowledge would have been different, but under whatever sky I had been born, since it is the same sky, I should have had the same philosophy.[2]

Santayana refers to "public experience" as all that is needed to "prove" his philosophical views. I take it that he

---

[2] George Santayana, *Skepticism and Animal Faith* (New York: Charles Scribner's Sons, 1923), pp. ix–x.

means by "public experience" what I have called "common experience," and that he is using the word "prove" in the sense in which it means "test." I would have added a few other things, but not many, to Santayana's enumeration of the things that belong to the core of common experience, such things as the multiplicity of separate bodies that come to be and pass away, that move about in space and change in other respects; the multiplicity of other persons with whom we communicate by language or other means; pleasures and pains; doubts and misgivings; memories of the past and anticipations of the future; sensing and knowing; sleeping, waking, and dreaming; growing old.

What Santayana calls "public experience" Professor Alfred North Whitehead calls "immediate experience" and Professor John Dewey calls "macroscopic experience," but the referent would appear to be the same.[3]

3

One more distinction must be mentioned in this process of placing philosophy properly in the picture that includes history, science, and mathematics as diverse modes of inquiry and distinct branches of knowledge. It is the distinction between first-order knowledge and knowledge of the second order.

Knowledge is of the first order if it is knowledge about reality, and of the second order if it is knowledge about knowledge itself. For example, the knowledge that a biologist has about the anatomy and physiology of living organisms is first-order knowledge, but the knowledge that a philosopher has about biology as a field of natural science and in relation

[3] See Whitehead's *Process and Reality* (New York and Cambridge: Macmillan, 1929), pp. 6, 7; and Dewey's *Experience and Nature* (Chicago and London: Open Court Publishing Co., 1925), pp. 2–10.

to the physical sciences on which it may depend is second-order knowledge.

This example not only explains the distinction between first- and second-order knowledge, but also tells us that philosophy as a branch of knowledge involves both first- and second-order knowledge. That is why it is associated with history and science in one respect and with mathematics in another.

It is, by the way, the only branch of knowledge that has a number of different dimensions, being first-order knowledge when it is engaged in metaphysics, the philosophy of nature, and of mind, and philosophical theology, as well as in moral and political philosophy; and second-order knowledge when it is engaged in the study of ideas and in the philosophy of other branches of knowledge and other forms of intellectual activity.

This is so important that I will devote the next chapter to a fuller statement of this most distinctive feature of philosophy—that it is the only branch of knowledge that belongs on both sides of the line of demarcation that separates history and science from mathematics, and that separates empirical modes of inquiry from formal modes of thought.

Extreme positivism of the Humean variety rejects philosophy entirely as a branch of knowledge, even in the moderate sense of that term. But a less extreme form of positivism, which has appeared in the twentieth century in the work of the analytical and linguistic philosophers, while rejecting metaphysics and moral philosophy as first-order knowledge, associates philosophy with mathematics and logic in the realm of second-order knowledge. In my judgment, that does not suffice to restore philosophy to its proper place in our culture, education, and lives with the self-respect and public esteem it deserves.

4

History is associated with empirical science in the realm of first-order knowledge. Like science, it is an investigative discipline that depends on the data of special experience, but it differs from science in the method its mode of inquiry employs. Pure historical research performs no experiments and collects no statistical arrays. Instead, it looks for and probes particular remains from the past; examines documents, traces, and monuments; sifts testimony, and the like. The conclusions of historical research are singular propositions about past events, persons, institutions, or movements. When historians generalize about the course of history, they become engaged, more or less explicitly, in the philosophy of history.

Similarly, when scientists (such as geologists, paleontologists, and evolutionists) sometimes attempt to establish the spatial and temporal determinants of particular past events or to describe a particular sequence of such events, they cease to be engaged in scientific inquiry and become engaged in historical research, sometimes called natural history.

Though both history and science are investigative modes of inquiry that submit their conclusions to the test of experience (i.e., the data obtained by investigation), history by its method can answer questions that science cannot answer; and science by its method can answer questions that history cannot answer.

To say that mathematics is armchair thinking or noninvestigative does not preclude dependence on experience. The mathematician has to get from somewhere his elementary notions or concepts—those that he subsequently uses to construct more elaborate and refined concepts. If these initial concepts are not innate, they must be experiential in origin. But the experience from which they originate is common experience, and the mathematician needs relatively little even of that. The existence of mathematical prodigies would suggest that mathematicians do not need more than the common experience enjoyed by the young.

Professor Popper's line of demarcation between statements that can and statements that cannot be falsified by appeal to experience perfectly separates empirical science and historical research, on the one hand, from mathematical thought, on the other hand. The objects of mathematics are not mutable, sensible, physical existents. This does not preclude mathematics from being applicable to the physical world. Physical measurements give us observed quantities, relations, orders, or sets that are capable of fitting into mathematical formulas by serving as constants substitutable for the variables in terms of which the mathematical formulas are constructed. The essential point is that the pure mathematician does not desist from his inquiries because he cannot foresee how these conclusions might be applied to physical phenomena.

In the realm of second-order knowledge, where philosophy is associated with mathematics as armchair thinking, philosophy also has a method and objects of its own that differentiate it from mathematics. Just as philosophy cannot answer the questions that are within the province of mathematics, so mathematics cannot answer the questions philosophy asks about the objects with which it is concerned in the realm of the second order.

CHAPTER 3

First and Second Intentions

I

Grammar and logic were two of the seven liberal arts that were cultivated in the Middle Ages and that achieved both subtlety and precision in their development. The twentieth-century distinction between first- and second-order knowledge has its roots in the mediaeval distinction between first and second intentions in acts of the mind. This is the logical parallel of the grammatical distinction between first and second impositions in the use of language.

When we use words to name things or, in conversation, use language to talk about the world in which we live, we are speaking in the first imposition. But when we use language to talk about language itself or use a word as the subject of some predication, then we are using language and words in the second imposition.

When I say the word "cat" to designate that feline mammal, I am using the word in the first imposition. But when, in another context, I say "cat is a noun," I am using the word "cat" in the second imposition; and, of course, the word "noun," which can only be used in speaking about words, is also in the second imposition, "cat" as subject and "noun" as predicate.

First and second intentions in thinking parallel first and second impositions in speaking or writing. When I think about human beings as, let us say, rational animals, I am thinking in the first intention, for the objects of my thought are really existent organisms. But when I think about human beings as a species that belongs in the class of vertebrate mammals, I am thinking in the second intention. All acts of taxonomic assignment are logical acts of thought and, therefore, in the second intention.

Another example may be helpful as well as specially pertinent. This book about philosophy involves a great deal of thinking in the second intention, but in the very next chapter, concerned with the philosophical presuppositions of what has so far been said about philosophy and science and other branches of knowledge, the major points will consist of thinking about reality and about the human mind in relation to reality. That will be thinking in the first intention.

Positivists who still continue to philosophize while denying that philosophical thought can achieve objectively valid knowledge of reality must do their work entirely in the domain of second intentions and second impositions. Unlike Hume, who could find no place for philosophy in his scheme of things, which includes only empirical science (concerned with matters of fact and real existence) and mathematics (which concerns the relation between objects of thought), twentieth-century positivists find a place for philosophy in the realm of second impositions and second intentions. That is why the work they do is called analytic and linguistic philosophy. Philosophy for them is exclusively second-order work, replacing the mediaeval vernacular by the jargon that is now current.

This view of philosophy associates it with mathematics on two counts, not one. Like mathematics, it is a noninvestigative mode of inquiry—armchair thinking. But it is also like mathematics in being second-order work, not knowledge of the physical world and the world of human affairs.

As a result, the questions that philosophy alone can answer when it is first-order knowledge must go unanswered, because they cannot be answered by historical research and by the empirical sciences.

2

When I wrote *The Conditions of Philosophy* almost thirty years ago, I claimed that philosophy as a mode of inquiry could answer questions that mathematics could not answer in the sphere of second-order knowledge, as well as being able to answer questions in the sphere of first-order knowledge that could not be answered by historical research or by the empirical sciences. What is most distinctive about philosophy in relation to all other recognized models of inquiry is its binary character—a mode of inquiry that can achieve knowledge in both the first and the second order.

To that extent, I anticipated the central message of this book—that philosophy was not one-dimensional in the kind of questions it alone can answer. But I did not foresee what I hope this book will clearly establish—that philosophy has four distinct dimensions, two in the realm of first-order inquiry and two in the realm of second-order inquiry.

Readers who now look back at this book's Contents will see that the first two dimensions are metaphysical and moral philosophy in first-order inquiry; and that in second-order inquiry, the third and fourth dimensions consist of the understanding of ideas and the understanding of subjects, such as the branches of knowledge and the other forms of intellectual work. This philosophical book about history, mathematics, science, and philosophy is philosophy in its fourth dimension.

Readers will have observed that Part Two of this book, dealing with the first and second dimensions of philosophy, refers to philosophy as *knowledge;* and that Part Three of this book, dealing with the third and fourth dimensions of philosophy, refers to philosophy as *understanding*. If this shift from knowledge to understanding puzzles them, I must ask them to wait for an explanation until subsequent chapters have prepared the way for it.

3

Here, then, in summary, are the questions to which we can find no answers unless philosophy as a mode of inquiry has a method for answering them.

A. IN THE FIRST ORDER

First Dimension: questions about being and the modes of being; questions about the being of the immaterial; questions about the existence of God; questions about the actual and the possible; questions about the human mind and human nature; questions about chance and necessity in the cosmos.

Second Dimension: questions about the good life and the good society; questions about our moral obligations with respect to justice, liberty, and equality; questions about democracy and socialism.

B. IN THE SECOND ORDER

Third Dimension: questions about ideas as objects of thought.

Fourth Dimension: questions about the branches of knowledge, the arts, the learned professions.

CHAPTER 4

Presuppositions

I

In the course of discussing knowledge in the preceding pages, the words "reality" and "experience" have frequently appeared; and in dealing with the distinction between first- and second-order knowledge, there have been references to the human mind and to ideas. These words and references raise philosophical problems—problems to which philosophers in modern times have given different answers and about which they have disputed.

A philosophical book about philosophy—or, for that matter, a philosophical book about science, mathematics, or history—is thus confronted by an embarrassment. How shall it deal with its own philosophical presuppositions?

To deal at length in this book with the philosophical controversies that surround them would involve writing several other books at the same time. That is impossible, not only for the writer but for the reader as well. The alternative, to which I think it prudent to take recourse, is a frank acknowledgment of the philosophical affirmations that have so far been presupposed and will in succeeding chapters continue to be presupposed.[1]

---

[1] As I said in *The Conditions of Philosophy* (1965), p. 73: "In place of expounding and defending at length the philosophical theories which are presupposed by the conception of philosophy here being advanced, I shall simply state, as briefly as possible without argument, the presuppositions to which I am committed. To present them in this way is merely to alert the reader to them. I should add that I regard them as fundamentally sound—much more tenable and truer than their contraries."

I stated the two main presuppositions—the first about reality and experience, the second about human nature and the human mind—in *The Conditions of Philosophy*. Since then, I have written a number of philosophical books that deal with the modern controversies concerning these matters, books in which I have stated views opposed to my own views, and argued for the doctrines I espouse. Footnote references to these books will enable readers to go beyond the brief summary presented here and better understand the pros and cons of the underlying presuppositions.

2

My first presupposition is a firm commitment to a view that is traditionally called realism. The opposite view, since the time of Immanuel Kant, has been called idealism, and in very recent philosophical literature has taken a new form and name—constructivist philosophy. Readers will be misled if they attach to the word "idealism" the moral, social, and political connotations it has in ordinary speech as the antithesis to realism. Idealism in philosophy is the denial of any knowable reality that is *independent* of the human mind and its ideas.

"Independent" is the critically operative word here. The alternatives are clear and exhaustive: either (1) there exists that which is both independent of the human mind and is also knowable by it or (2) everything that is knowable is mind-dependent. Idealists claim that if there is anything completely independent of the human mind, it is unknowable. Kant affirms the reality of things in themselves, *Dinge an sich*, but at the same time dismisses them as unknowable.

The word "reality" can, therefore, be simply defined as that which is totally independent of the human mind. It exists whether we think about it or not. It has whatever characteristics it has regardless of how we think about it. In addition, it is knowable by the human mind, and the truth we have in our minds when we know it consists in the correspondence between what we think about it and the way it is—a correspondence between our minds and reality.

This last point asserts that our theories or conclusions can be falsified by something that is extrinsic to and independent of our minds. It provides us with a basis for determining whether our efforts to know reality fail or succeed.

The man of common sense is an unquestioning realist. I presume that all or most readers of this book, at least those who are not professors of philosophy, are commonsense realists. The idealistic tendencies of modern thought are at variance with the commonsense views that most of us live and act by. As I have written elsewhere,

> Our inveterate realism is, perhaps, best illustrated by what goes on in a courtroom when a jury renders a verdict in answer to questions of fact that are being put on trial. Our business transactions as well as our freedom from fines and imprisonment, even death in capital cases, depend on our acceptance of a jury's verdict that certain things are true or false with sufficient probability to be relied upon.
>
> In the world of real existences, the jury's verdict is that this probably did happen and that probably did not. We accept without question that there is a reality to be known with probability, not certitude. We also accept without question that the testimony that reports the experience of witnesses enables us to know with sufficient probability what really happened.
>
> What I have just said about the conduct of a jury trial applies to almost all the commerical transactions in which we engage. The questions to be resolved in such transactions are almost always questions about what really is or is not the case.[2]

---

[2] *Intellect: Mind Over Matter* (New York: Macmillan, 1990; paperback edition, 1993), p. 87. For my arguments against idealism and constructivist philosophy, see Chapters 7 and 9 there.

This commonsense realism, which betrays naiveté in certain respects, philosophical realism corrects and critically refines. As I said before, the idealism it opposes cannot be found in either ancient or mediaeval philosophy. Idealism is an error exclusively modern.

Before I turn to the second presupposition that is a basic commitment of this book, I would like to outline briefly the scope of the reality with which philosophy is concerned, only certain parts of which are also the concern of the natural and social sciences and of history.

It would be a serious mistake to suppose that reality is confined to the physical world, the phenomena of which are observable by the investigative natural sciences and by what is traditionally called natural history. To deny that the cosmos or this planet is independent of the human mind that claims to have empirically verifiable knowledge of it is to deny that claim, for if the existence of the cosmos or this earth were dependent on the existence of the human mind then the great antiquity that scientists and natural historians attribute to it must be false. If their existence is dependent on the human mind then their age is no greater than that of the human species *Homo sapiens,* approximately forty-five thousand years ago.

The scope of reality includes the human world in every aspect of it that is studied by cultural anthropologists and by social and political historians, as well as by moral and political philosophers. It is even more extensive then, for as approached by philosophy, especially by metaphysical inquiries and by philosophical psychology and theology, it goes beyond the reach of historical research and the investigative natural and social sciences. It considers questions about immaterial and, therefore, suprasensible realities. The immaterial realm of being, dogmatically denied by materialists, is an intelligible but not a sensible realm of being, and so cannot be investigated by the modes of empirical inquiry.

Theoretical physicists such as Stephen Hawking have gone beyond their authority in denying the reality of the immaterial. Albert Einstein once said that what cannot be measured by the physicist has no significance for physicists. But what has no interest for their empiriometric mode of inquiry should not lead to the denial of the reality that is studied by history, the social sciences, and philosophy. Yet that denial is to be found in Hawking's *A Brief History of Time*. He goes further than Einstein in asserting, with impudent arrogance, that what is not measurable by physicists *does not exist in reality.*[3]

Both commonsense realism and the critical realism of philosophy hold that existence can be attributed to the human mind, including its subjective states of consciousness. To each of us, without investigation, the reality of his or her own mind is evident. Each of us also acknowledges the reality of minds in other human beings.

These real existences are suprasensible. We have no perceptual experience of them. But that is no ground for denying their reality. In short, reality extends beyond the realm of the sensible to the realm of that which is intelligible, the real existence of which can be known by inference, even if it is not an object of sense-perception.

3

A point to which I called attention in my statement of the first presupposition leads into the second. It was that reality includes intelligible objects that are suprasensible, and also that the sensible reality of the physical world is intelligible to us. Empirical physical science is more than a description of sensible phenomena. It provides us with some understanding of the physical world, an understanding that is incomplete and

[3] See my book *Truth in Religion: The Plurality of Religions and the Unity of Truth* (New York: Macmillan, 1990), pp. 14, 71.

needs to be supplemented by a philosophy of nature and by metaphysics, but an understanding nevertheless. To the extent that anything is understandable, it is intelligible.

If reality is intelligible to us, our minds must include an intellectual power distinct from and superior to the whole array of sensitive powers—our perceptual, imaginative, and memorative powers that are rooted in our brain and central nervous system.

One of the most grievous mistakes in modern philosophy is its denial of the intellect and its reduction of our cognitive powers to those that operate through the senses, memory, and imagination. This led the British philosophers Hobbes, Locke, Berkeley, and Hume to the self-refuting nominalism of denying our possession of what they called abstract ideas and giving inadequate accounts of the empirical sciences and the mathematics that they deem to be genuine knowledge. Locke and Hume use the word "understanding" in the titles of their books (the English translation of the Greek word *nous*), even though their psychological account of the mind's operations is entirely in terms of sense-perceptions and sensitive memories and images.

In my view, any attempt to explain the nature of philosophical knowledge of reality without affirming the human intellect as distinct from the senses must fail miserably. This applies also to philosophy's analytical response to second-order questions. Hence, this second presupposition must be added to the first.[4]

If I were to add a third presupposition, it would be to correct another serious mistake of very recent origin. In the twentieth century, existentialists and cultural anthropologists have denied that human beings have a genetically determined specific nature. What has been said about the common core

[4]For an exposition of arguments to support this second presupposition, see Chapter 2 on "The Intellect and the Senses," in *Ten Philosophical Mistakes;* and also *Intellect: Mind Over Matter,* Prologue and Chapters 3, 4, and 5.

of human experience and how it functions in relation to philosophical thought requires us to presuppose that the human mind is the same everywhere and at all times.

Man's determinate nature remains constant as long as man remains an identifiable and definable species of living organism. All the social and cultural influences that mold our development through the processes by which we are nurtured and conditioned operate on a determinate set of potentialities that constitute the inherent properties of specific human nature—the specific nature of *Homo sapiens*.[5]

---

[5] For a fuller statement of the argument against the denial of human nature, see my book *Ten Philosophical Mistakes*, Chapter 8; and *Haves Without Have-Nots: Essays for the 21st Century on Democracy* (New York: Macmillan, 1991), Chapter 5 on "Human Nature, Nurture, and Culture."

CHAPTER 5

Tests of Truth
in Philosophy

I

The definition of truth as the correspondence of the mind with reality presupposes philosophical realism. Idealists denying a reality independent of the mind lack anything independent of the mind to serve as its measure.

To avoid a confusion that runs through philosophical controversies about truth, it must be remembered that the correspondence theory of truth is not itself a test of truth. It merely states the definition of truth—what it is. This underlies all the empirical and pragmatic tests of truth. As we shall see, the logical tests of truth, such as coherence or the absence of intrinsic contradiction in a theory, do not presuppose the realist's definition of truth as agreement or conformity of our thinking with the way things, in fact, are. That is why idealists tend to define truth entirely in terms of coherence.

The definition of truth in terms of correspondence does not apply to the whole of philosophy, first because in the sphere of second-order knowledge, philosophical analysis, like mathematics, does not consist in thinking about matters of fact and real existences; and secondly, because it applies only to propositions that are descriptive and not to propositions that are prescriptive.

Let me explain the distinction between descriptive and prescriptive propositions. A descriptive proposition is one which asserts that something exists or has certain properties or attributes. It asserts that that which is, is; or that that which is not, is not. Obviously, such assertions correspond to that which is or is not. The contrary assertions—the denial that that which is, is, or the the affirmation that that which is, is not—obviously do not correspond and, therefore, are false. But prescriptive propositions—propositions that declare what ought to be sought, desired, or chosen, or what ought to be avoided, not desired, nor chosen—have no reality with which to correspond.

In what sense, then, can they either be true or false? The failure to find an answer to this question has resulted in the twentieth-century view of ethics as *noncognitive*—that is, not a branch of objective valid knowledge.

An answer is to be found in one sentence in Chapter 2 of the sixth book of Aristotle's *Ethics* and appears to be known only to some of his later disciples. There Aristotle points out that the truth of injunctions (which contain the words "ought" and "ought not") cannot correspond to reality. Their truth, he writes, consists in their conformity to right desire.

This is not the place to explain how this definition of prescriptive truth works in moral and political philosophy and serves to establish them as objectively valid branches of knowledge.[1] I mention it here only to indicate the limited applicability of the correspondence definition of truth: not to prescriptive knowledge, as we have just seen, and also not to second intentional, or second-order, philosophical analysis.[2]

One further preliminary clarification is necessary before

---

[1] The explanation will be forthcoming in Part Two, Chapter 9.

[2] This second limitation of the correspondence definition of truth will be discussed in Part Three.

we consider the various tests of truth. Strictly speaking, the correspondence definition of truth applies to propositions that are entertained by the mind with suspended judgment. These are either true or false and immutably so; nor do we ever say of them that they are in the sphere of doubt. They are either true or false but never more or less probable.[3]

When judgment is not suspended, and the mind judges correctly or incorrectly about the truth or falsity of propositions under consideration, such judgments may be either highly probable (i.e., beyond a reasonable doubt) or just more probable than contrary judgments, but they are never beyond the shadow of a doubt. They change from time to time, as new empirical evidence is found or new and better reasons are given for altered judgments.

If we never applied the words "truth" and "falsity" to such judgments, but always spoke of them as "correct" or "incorrect," we would not have to say that when we refer to such judgments as true or false, as we habitually do in every-day speech, the correspondence definition of truth applies to them differently from the way it applies to propositions that are entertained with suspended judgment.

In the case of judgments, their truth consists in *correctly affirming as true* propositions that are true because they correspond with reality. When we incorrectly judge a proposition that is true to be false (as great physical scientists did with respect to the divisibility of atoms), then instead of saying that our judgment is incorrect, we say that it is false. In other words, truth and falsity as said of our correct and incorrect judgments is truth and falsity by one remove from correspondence with reality.

[3] An example of such an immutable and certain truth is the proposition that atoms are divisible into elementary particles. The production of atomic fission in this century falsifies the proposition that was judged to be true (i.e., that atoms are indivisible units of matter) by philosophers and physical scientists from Greek antiquity down to the fourth quarter of the nineteenth century.

2

Tests of truth are either empirical or pragmatic or they are logical. In both cases, our sensitive powers and our rational processes may be involved, but in tests that are empirical and pragmatic, sensory experience, usually perceptual, is indispensable.

The empirical and pragmatic test of truth clearly derives from the correspondence definition of it. Let us suppose that you find yourself asleep in a hotel room that has three doors, one to the hallway, one to a clothes closet, and one to the bathroom. You awaken, fail to turn on the light, and wanting to go to the bathroom, your thinking about which door opens into the bathroom turns out to be incorrect or false. How did you find that out? By opening the wrong door and bumping your head against clothes in the closet. Your false or incorrect judgment has been tested by your action. Your action does not work out successfully.

Idealist philosophers in the time of William James, such as F. H. Bradley of Oxford, vilified him for defining truth pragmatically as that which works successfully or pays off in action. They failed to understand that James was offering a pragmatic test of truth, not a definition of it, which, for him, consisted in correspondence with reality.

Another empirical test of truth is offered by Professor Karl Popper. It applies to all generalizations in science or philosophy; that is, statements that contain the word "all" or "always." In his view, the test of truth with regard to such statements is to be found empirically in the perception of one or more negative instances.

The judgment that all swans are white is falsified by one negative instance—the perceptual experience of one black swan. Generalizations that time and time again are exposed to the possibility of falsification by contrary perceptual experience and escape such falsification are correctly judged by us to be true with an increasing degree of probability, but they never attain certitude. They always remain in the sphere of doubt. They are never beyond the shadow of a doubt.[4]

3

Of the four tests of truth in philosophy, only two are empirical. They are applicable to science as well as to philosophy. They are, as we have seen, the pragmatic test of whether a judgment, leading to action on our part, has a successful outcome; and the test of generalizations—whether or not the generalizations are falsified by the perception of one or more negative instances.

All the remaining tests are logical, and here the principle of inner coherence, not correspondence with reality, is operative. Nevertheless, the correspondence definition of truth is still presupposed because the principle of noncontradiction (which governs coherence) is an ontological as well as a logical principle. In other words, coherence, or the absence of contradiction, is a sign of truth in our thinking because there are no contradictions in reality. Hence only a coherent theory or doctrine can correspond with reality.[5]

When in the claims to truth made by historians, scientists, or philosophers, incoherence is found by virtue of some incompatibility among the elements of what is being proposed for consideration, the remedy, of course, is the elimination of one or the other of the incompatible elements, thus resolving

[4] That is why, with the exception of a small number of self-evident truths that do have certitude, philosophical knowledge is not what the Greeks thought of as *epistēmē*, but rather what they thought of as *doxa*—knowledge that remains in the sphere of doubt.

[5] For the defense of this against the Copenhagen interpretation of Heisenberg's principle of indeterminacy in quantum mechanics, see my book *Six Great Ideas*, pp. 212–18; and also my *Truth in Religion*: Note to Chapter 4 on reality in relation to quantum theory, pp. 93–100.

the contradiction. It is in this way that hypotheses, theories, or doctrines are logically corrigible and amendable, becoming thereby not just true, but truer than they had been before.

The most all-embracing of all applications of the principle of coherence is the one that applies to branches of first-order knowledge. In this application, the principle affirms the unity of truth. This, fully understood, declares that all the branches of human knowledge are interdependent. Consequently, even though each branch has its own mode of inquiry and method that enables it to answer certain questions and not others, thereby possessing autonomy, that autonomy is relative and limited, not absolute.

Truth is a whole that has many parts, parts that differ from one branch of knowledge to another by virtue of each branch's mode of inquiry and method of posing and answering questions. We may even include in this whole of truth a part that consists in the dogmas of religious faith, but only, of course, if factual-logical truth is claimed by a religion.

The different modes of inquiry and the different methods of the relatively autonomous branches of knowledge do not exempt them from the application of the principle of coherence. Something cannot be claimed to be true in philosophy or religion that is inconsistent with what is claimed to be true in history or science. The fact that history and science cannot answer the questions that fall within the province of philosophy's mode of inquiry and its method does not exempt it from being challenged and discredited by knowledge available to history or science.

How can this be, it may be wondered, if the questions to be answered are purely philosophical? To say that a question is purely philosophy is to say that it can be answered only by philosophy's mode of inquiry. Hence if history or science cannot answer such questions, how can they challenge or discredit the answers given by philosophy?

The solution is twofold. First, in the case of purely philosophical questions, the answer given may include assertions about matters of fact that fall within the purview of science. Secondly, not all the questions that philosophy tries to answer are purely philosophical. Some are mixed questions, falling within the province of both science and philosophy. Let me now give examples of these two cases.

4

The question whether a spiritual Supreme Being exists is clearly a purely philosophical question. The attempt to prove or disprove that God exists is entirely a philosophical effort. But let us suppose that one of the premises in the argument attempting to prove God's existence is a proposition asserting that the cosmos is radically contingent. It is capable of not being. One indication of this is that it is capable of being otherwise than it is. The crucial proposition in the proof of God's existence as the exnihilating cause of a radically contingent cosmos is the statement that what is capable of being otherwise is capable of not being at all.

The truth of this philosophical statement may be beyond a reasonable doubt, but it certainly is not beyond the shadow of a doubt. The question of fact involved—the question of whether chance, randomness, and contingency are present in this cosmos—is a question about which the natural sciences, biology as well as physics, have something to say.

I think they confirm the radical contingency of the cosmos, but others may think the opposite; and if, at a given time, the received opinion among scientists competent to judge is that this cosmos is not capable of being otherwise (that, in fact, it is necessarily determined to be the way it is), then it follows that a proof of God's existence that has been developed in philosophical theology has been, to that extent, discredited; and philosophical theology must get to work revising its proof.

5

For an example of a mixed question involving both empirical science and philosophy, let us turn from theology to philosophical psychology. The question, which both empirical and philosophical psychology try to answer, is about the intellect in relation to the brain.

There is no question that all the sensory powers of the human mind, as well as the minds of brute animals, are seated in bodily organs. We cannot see without having healthy eyes to see with, and we also see with them. The visual apparatus along with its connections in the cerebral cortex is the bodily organ of vision. But is the brain the bodily organ of intellectual thought? Not if we do not think with our brains, even though we cannot think without them.

The opposite philosophical answer is the materialist answer, either denying that the intellect is radically distinct from all our sensitive powers or asserting that conceptual thought is an activity of the human brain. This answer is given not only by philosophers who are materialists, but also by neurophysiologists, experimental psychologists, and experts in the field of artificial intelligence.

At the moment, the issue remains unresolved. But the great computer expert A. M. Turing proposed a way to test whether artificial intelligence machines can think in a completely human way. The test involves asking a human being and an AI machine, both behind a screen, a long series of questions. The AI machine and the human being are instructed to try to deceive the interrogator. If the AI machine succeeds in doing this, so that the interrogator can find no discernible difference between the answers given by the human being and the AI machine, then, according to Turing, we are justified in concluding that a machine has been built that can think in a thoroughly human fashion. Since the machine is built out of entirely material parts, the immaterialist answer must be dismissed as false.

At present computer technicians have not yet built a machine that can successfully pass the Turing test. So far they have tried and failed, but they can try again. Each time they try and fail it becomes more and more probable that the immaterialist position in philosophical psychology is the correct solution to the issue about the intellect in relation to the brain.

The future is long and unpredictable. The philosophical arguments for the immaterialist position are strong, but that position will always remain in the realm of doubt. The continued failure of the computer technologists to produce an artificial intelligence machine that can pass the Turing test increases the probability that the position of the philosophical immaterialist is true, or at least truer than the position taken by its adversaries.[6]

6

It may be asked why, when conflicts occur between empirical science and philosophy, the resolution of them tends to favor science. It is on the side of science, not philosophy, that we tend to think that the more probable truth lies. Why?

Let us remember that while both science and philosophy appeal to experience, science is investigative and philosophy is not. The experience that philosophy appeals to is the common core of everyday experience that everyone shares, whereas scientific investigation turns up specialized experience—the data gathered by investigative observation, usually aided by powerful instrumentation.

That is why we tend to favor the conclusions reached by investigative science and allow conclusions it has established at a given time to discredit philosophical assertions with

---

[6]See my *Intellect: Mind Over Matter*, Chapters 4 and 5.

which they are incompatible. However, the interdependence of science and philosophy works both ways. Scientists as well as philosophers make mistakes that the others correct. The mistakes usually consist in philosophers or scientists erroneously exceeding an authority that is limited—limited by their mode of inquiry and the method they employ to answer questions within their province and nothing outside it.

This interdependence has worked in opposite directions in different epochs. In antiquity and the Middle Ages, philosophers could not possibly have foreseen the extraordinary discoveries that would be made by scientific investigation in modern times, from the seventeenth century to the present day. Such ignorance on their part may be excusable, but it led them to exceed their rightful authority by venturing to answer questions beyond their powers because investigation was needed to answer them. They should have waited for science to answer them later.

An example of this is Aristotle's wrong answer concerning the difference between the matter of celestial and terrestrial bodies. His answer was based on the common human experience of the heavens observed without telescopes and other means of scientific observation. Another example is the wrong answer given by Descartes concerning force and momentum in the physics of moving bodies.

On the other hand, in modern times empirical scientists who are philosophically ignorant or naive presume to make statements that their mode of inquiry does not give them the authority to assert. For example, in twentieth-century cosmology many physicists of eminence have asserted that the big bang 18 billion years ago can be interpreted as the beginning of the cosmos and of time, when they should have said more precisely that it is for them the beginning of a physically measurable cosmos and of measurable time.

Some even go so far as to talk about creation without having understood that creation is exnihilation. They proceed in ignorance of philosophical theology and do not know that any discussion of creation must assume a cosmos without a beginning or an end in time, and that creation must be understood as making something out of nothing. It is not just an explosive transformation of the state in which matter exists—the so-called big bang. Here, then, it is the philosopher who has the authority to correct a mistake made by those scientists who have strayed beyond their sphere of competence.

7

The principle of coherence also operates as a test of truth in a way that is peculiar to philosophy. The reason this is so is that only philosophy claims to have a hold on truth in different modes—the descriptive mode of *is* or *is not* statements (which it shares with science) and the prescriptive mode of *ought* or *ought not* statements (only within the province of philosophy to assert). In *The Conditions of Philosophy,* I called this the "is-ought" test of truth.

In that book I gave the following example of how this test works. I wrote:

> Does a philosopher's view of the nature of things support or undermine his view of how men should conduct their lives? In the one case, he would be free from inconsistency; in the other, not. For example, a philosopher who denies the existence of individual beings which retain their identity over a span of time cannot consistently hold that men should be held morally responsible for acts which they performed at an earlier time. If there are no such enduring entities, the agent who performed a certain act at an earlier time cannot be identical with the individual who is to be charged at a later time with moral responsibility for that act.[7]

Another example is that of the determinist who denies that human beings have free choice and yet, when he comes

_____
[7] *The Conditions of Philosophy,* pp. 195–96.

to prescribing human conduct, makes statements about how they ought to behave. It has been said that "ought implies can." If injunctions about how we ought to behave are true, then it must also be true that we freely choose to obey those injunctions or to violate them. Such inconsistencies cannot be resolved by taking either horn of the dilemma and retracting that statement. The *ought* has a prior claim on our allegiance.

Our common experience of living and acting gives a certain primacy to prescriptive over descriptive truth. The denial of moral responsibility is immediately falsified by our common experience of human life, in which we feel responsible for our acts and hold others responsible for theirs. The primacy of the prescriptive over the descriptive gives special force to the "is-ought" test. It requires us to reject as unsound any philosophical theory about what *is* or *is not* which undermines our effort, on the prescriptive side, to deal philosophically with how men *ought* to behave.

8

Still other examples of internal inconsistency in philosophical thought raise questions about which of the incompatible views should prevail.

A sound philosophical theory should be free from internal inconsistencies or theoretical embarrassments. Their presence indicates serious flaws or defects—some mixing of error and truth. The "swerve of the atoms," invoked by Lucretius to explain free will, is a scandalous embarrassment to a theory that attempts to explain everything in mechanical terms. The necessity for psychophysical interaction to explain sensation and voluntary movement is an equally scandalous embarrassment to the Cartesian theory of mind and body as separate substances. Bishop Berkeley's introduction of "notions" to account for our knowledge of spiritual beings is inconsistent with his basic principle that *all* the objects of human knowledge are "either ideas actually imprinted on the senses, or else such as are perceived by attending to the passions and operations of the mind, or lastly, ideas formed by the help of memory and imagination." The mind, soul, or spirit that knows or perceives is not itself an object of knowledge and cannot be, since we can have no idea of it. Nevertheless, Berkeley is compelled to assert that "we have some *notion* of soul, spirit . . . inasmuch as we know or understand the meaning of these words."

Berkeley also affords us another example of internal inconsistency, one that is present in all nominalist attempts to account for "general ideas," or the meaning of common names, while at the same time denying the existence of abstract ideas. The bishop finds himself forced to say that "an idea which, considered in itself, is particular becomes general by being made to represent or stand for all other particular ideas of the same sort." The nominalist's embarrassment lies in the impossibility of his explaining how we can know that two or more particular ideas are "of the same sort" when we can have no idea whatsoever of any sorts or kinds.

The nominalist's inability to escape inconsistency appears in another way in Hume. The "absurdity of all scholastic notions with regard to abstraction and general ideas," he tells us, will be seen by anyone who tries "to conceive a triangle in general, which is neither *Isosceles* nor *Scalenum,* nor has any particular length or proportion of sides." But when, in another place, he treats mathematics, he tell us that "though there never were a circle or triangle in nature, the truths demonstrated by Euclid would forever retain their certainty and evidence." He offers as an example the proposition about the equality between the square on the hypotenuse of a right triangle and the sum of the squares on the other two sides; but he overlooks the fact, as he must, that this geometrical theorem applies to *all* right triangles, regardless of the length of the sides; and he must ignore the fact that other Euclidean theorems deal with the properties of triangles in general (prescinding from the special properties of triangles which are equilateral, scalene, or isosceles). How geometry can treat such objects when it is impossible for us to conceive of them is a matter that the nominalist must always find embarrassing to explain.

Still one more example of an embarrassing inconsistency is to be found in the ethical theory of the Roman Stoics. On the one hand, central to their doctrine is the proposition that nothing which happens to you from external sources can injure you if you interpret it as not doing so. On the other hand, the Stoics say the virtuous man will be just to others and refrain from injuring them. But injustice on the part of one individual to another is impossible if he cannot be injured by what impinges on him from without.[8]

9

Let us pass now from philosophical doctrines to philosophical analysis—from first to second intentions. In the sphere of thinking about thinking itself—not thinking about objects in the external sensible world but thinking about objects of thought and about the branches of knowledge and other products of intellectual work—the correspondence theory of truth does not apply. Coherence or logical consistency still remains an applicable test of truth, but by itself it is not enough to measure the worth or excellence of the philosophical effort.

One effort to understand ideas or objects of thought is better than another to the extent that it achieves clarity and comprehensiveness. Clear and adequate understanding has, in the sphere of second intentional thinking, an excellence that is appropriate to that sphere of thinking. It is the coun-

[8] See the *Encheiridion* of Epictetus.

terpart of truth by correspondence with reality in the sphere of first intentional thinking.

Mathematicians use the words "simple" and "elegant" for proofs, arguments, or formulations that they wish to praise. Philosophers might borrow these terms from mathematics and regard simplicity and elegance, along with clarity and adequacy, as the criteria of excellence in the case of philosophical work to which the criteria of truth do not apply.

Returning once more to philosophical doctrines that claim truth for themselves, it is important to remember that the philosophical knowledge with which we are dealing is *doxa,* not *epistēmē*—that is, it is knowledge in the sphere of doubt, never knowledge beyond the shadow of a doubt. To regard knowledge as in the sphere of doubt does not amount to a skeptical denial of knowledge.

Since such knowledge is always corrigible and amendable, we should never claim for a philosophical doctrine, as it is formulated at a given time, that it is true. To call it true smacks of a finality and incorrigibility that it does not possess. It would, therefore, be better to make the more modest claim that, at a given time, it is truer than competing alternatives, always bearing in mind that at a later time it may become truer or less true relative to alternative philosophical doctrines.

CHAPTER 6

Philosophy and Common Sense

I

Empirical science and historical research—both investigative modes of inquiry—add to what we know by common sense about the world in which we live and about its past. The reason this is so should be obvious at once. Both empirical science and historical research, being modes of inquiry that are investigative in their methods, appeal to special experience—the observed data that these modes of inquiry use for the development of scientific and historical knowledge.

Commonsense knowledge does not arise in that way. It develops out of the core of our common human experience. Hence commonsense knowledge is inadequate and imperfect knowledge of the knowable reality. Not only do science and history give us a much more extensive and elaborate knowledge of that same reality, but they also correct the errors in some of the opinions held by common sense.

In antiquity and the Middle Ages, man's observation of the movement of the heavenly bodies led to false opinions widely held. Investigative astronomy, with the aid of telescopic instruments, later corrected these mistakes. The same fate befell the widely held opinion that the earth was flat.

Here, too, investigation, going beyond common experience, corrected the error. One other commonsense error that investigative biology corrected was the opinion that living organisms were produced from putrefying matter by spontaneous generation.

2

The relation of philosophy to common sense is different from the relation to it of the investigative modes of inquiry.

In the first place, like commonsense knowledge, philosophical knowledge (i.e., *doxa,* opinions supported by evidence and reasons) is attained without investigation of any sort, mainly by intellectual insights and rational processes that have their empirical basis in our common human experience. As we have seen, it is corrigible and amendable, always in the realm of doubt, never with certitude beyond the shadow of a doubt.

But where empirical science and historical research go beyond commonsense knowledge and correct it when it is at fault, philosophy goes beyond it by refining, enlightening, and elaborating the truths known by common sense in the light of common experience. Hence, it might be said that philosophy is continuous with common sense, as empirical science and historical research are not.

Philosophical thought, when it is properly conducted (which has, for the most part, not been the case in modern times), never repudiates common sense, even when it may correct or refine some few particulars. When philosophy judges commonsense opinions to be sound, its rational and analytical processes contribute an understanding of the known facts that common sense rarely has.

Commonsense knowledge never serves as a test of the truth to be found in the conclusions of scientific investigation and of historical research. It cannot do so because these conclusions are based on the special experience—the observed data—not accessible to common sense. But when philosophical theories or conclusions come into conflict with common-sense knowledge, that inconsistency acts as a challenge to the philosophical doctrines in question. In consequence, the philosophical doctrine may need correction.

Let me give some examples of this. I pointed out earlier that common sense affirms the existence of a reality that is independent of the human mind and that measures the success or failure of our efforts to make our thinking about reality correspond to the way things really are or are not.[1] Though the conflict between philosophy and common sense is prevalent in modern times, it is found also in antiquity.

A thesis proposed by Plato's Socrates is clearly contrary to our common experience and our common sense. It is the Socratic doctrine that knowledge is virtue—that a person who knows what is right will inexorably do what is right. This is patently false, as everyone who has ever experienced remorse or regret for having committed an act that he or she knew at the time to be wrong, but nevertheless performed the action. Aristotle, criticizing the Platonic error, explains the human incontinence that allows this to happen.[2]

Aristotle's correction of the errors made by his teacher Plato almost always involves a defense of common sense against philosophical mistakes. I have often quoted Alfred North Whitehead's statement that the history of Western philosophy is largely a series of footnotes to the dialogues of Plato, always adding that Aristotle wrote most of the footnotes.

---

[1] See my book *Intellect: Mind Over Matter*, pp. 86–89, for an exposition of the inveterate realism of common sense. See also Chapter 7 in that book, on philosophy and common sense, especially pp. 80–83 for a statement of the conflict between common sense and the various forms of modern philosophical thought.

[2] See my book *Desires, Right & Wrong: The Ethics of Enough* (New York: Macmillan, 1991), Chapter 6, pp. 105–107.

Another philosophical mistake that philosophical thought in harmony with common sense rejects is the dualism of body and mind (or soul) to be found in Plato and Descartes. Here philosophy proposes a view of human beings that is contrary to the commonsense view of the unity of the human person. That unity is denied by the view that body and mind are two completely separate substances, yet somehow interactive. The unintelligibility of this generated all the insoluble riddles of the mind-body problem which have plagued philosophy since Descartes's dualism of *res extensa and res cogitans.*[3]

Another example of philosophy in conflict with common sense is the doctrine of causal determinism, with its denial of human free will. Parents who try to form a good moral character in their offspring exhort them to modify their behavior when they do wrong, assuring them that, if they had only exercised their willpower, they could have done otherwise than they did. Free choice is the ability always to choose otherwise, no matter what one chooses at a given time.

3

A few philosophers in this century have carried on their work in the light of common experience and a sound view of common sense.

One, as we have already seen, is George Santayana.[4] To Santayana's statement quoted earlier, I would like to add another statement by him, as follows:

I think that common sense, in a rough dogged way, is technically sounder than the special schools of philosophy, each of which squints and overlooks half the facts and half the diffi-

---

[3] The familiar textbook syllogism "All men are mortal, Socrates is a man, therefore, Socrates is mortal" becomes a piece of false reasoning if only Socrates's body is mortal while his soul is immortal. The syllogism is correct reasoning only if the statement that Socrates is a man refers to one reality, not to two separate and separable realities.

[4] See Chapter 2, p. 12, *supra.*

culties in its eagerness to find in some detail the key to the whole. I am animated by distrust of all high guesses, and by sympathy with the old prejudices and workaday opinions of mankind: they are ill expressed, but they are well grounded.[5]

Professor G. E. Moore of Cambridge University is another commonsense philosopher. I refer to his classic defense, against skepticism, of our commonsense knowledge about the existence of such things as my own body, bodies other than my own, the past, other minds, and so on.[6]

Of course, it is Aristotle who is preeminently the commonsense philosopher. In 1978, I wrote *Aristotle for Everybody*. I would like to quote here the opening passage in my Introduction to that book.

> Why Aristotle?
> Why for everybody?
> And why is an exposition of Aristotle for everybody an introduction to common sense?
> I can answer these three questions better after I have answered one other. Why philosophy? Why should everyone learn how to think philosophically—how to ask the kind of searching questions that children and philosophers ask and that philosophers sometimes answer?
> I have long been of the opinion that philosophy is everybody's business—but not in order to get more information about the world, our society, and ourselves. For that purpose, it would be better to turn to the natural and the social sciences and to history. It is in another way that philosophy is useful—to help us to understand things we already know, understand them better than we now understand them. That is why I think everyone should learn how to think philosophically.
> For that purpose, there is no better teacher than Aristotle. I do not hesitate to recommend him as the teacher to begin with. The only other teacher that I might have chosen is Plato, but in

[5] Santayana, *Skepticism and Animal Faith*, p. v.
[6] See G. E. Moore, "A Defence of Common Sense," in *Contemporary British Philosophy, First and Second Series* (London, 1924), pp. 193–208.

my judgment he is second best. Plato raised almost all the questions that everyone should face; Aristotle raised them too; and, in addition, gave us clearer answers to them. Plato taught Aristotle how to think philosophically, but Aristotle learned the lesson so well that he is the better teacher for all of us.[7]

4

When philosophy gets out of touch with common sense, as has happened strikingly in modern times, its doctrines tend to become esoteric, if not outlandish. When this happens, philosophical discourse becomes filled with technical jargon, each philosopher specializing in his own set of made-up terms.

Philosophical discourse, when it is in touch with common sense and harmonious with it, has no need whatsoever for any special jargon. It might even be said that philosophical discourse that uses the words of everyday speech reveals its affinity with common sense, for the words of everyday speech are the words that commonsense individuals employ in communicating with one another.

However, while the avoidance of all technical jargon in philosophical discourse is a desideratum, recourse to the vocabulary of everyday speech must be accompanied by great precision in the use of its words.

The words of everyday speech are used with great ambiguity, in many senses, often loose and ill-defined ones. One very special contribution that philosophy can make to common sense is to refine the use of the words of everyday speech by eliminating equivocations and calling sharp attention to the precise sense—one or more—in which a word is being used.

Philosophical discourse thus illuminates and elevates everyday speech, and in doing so, philosophy refines, elaborates, and enlightens common sense.

[7] *Aristotle for Everybody: Difficult Thought Made Easy* (New York: Macmillan, 1978; paperback edition, 1991), pp. ix–x.

CHAPTER 7

Science and Philosophy

I

We live in a culture in which science, along with its applications in ever more powerful technology, predominates. That is, perhaps, the most distinctive mark of the twentieth century. The glorification and adulation of science give the word "scientific" its eulogistic connotation. Other forms of intellectual endeavor call themselves "scientific" when, in fact, their mode of inquiry, which may be investigative, is not scientific at all in method or aim. The adjective "scientific" has almost become a synonym for "excellent"—for "trustworthy" and "reliable."

Under these pervasive cultural circumstances, philosophy takes a back seat. It either does not try to compete with scientific knowledge in the sphere of first-order questions, occupying itself with the processes of logical and linguistic analyses in the sphere of second-order questions; or it weakly claims for itself the eminence it once had in antiquity and the Middle Ages, an eminence that it no longer deserves in view of the numerous grave mistakes made by philosophers since the seventeenth century. A telling sign of philosophy's great disrepute at present is the fact that, of the 8,730 philanthropic foundations in the United States, *not one* lists philosophy among the guidelines for its giving.

In this chapter I am going to defend philosophy against the charges that are usually brought against it by those who unfairly compare it with the achievements of science since early modern times.

I am going to ignore the fact that, in this epoch in which science has advanced steadily, philosophy has declined steadily. I am going to proceed on the assumption that the ten or twelve grave errors made by modern philosophers can be and have been corrected; that philosophy has regained the courage to seek knowledge—both descriptive and prescriptive—about reality, returning from analytic work in the second order to metaphysical and moral philosophy in the first order; and that philosophy has a future in which its decline in the last three centuries can be reversed.

Even with these assumptions, it is necessary for us to consider the charges against philosophy that are currently rampant, not only in the academic mind, but in the popular mind as well. In my view, all or most of these charges overlook the differences between science and philosophy as distinct modes of inquiry. They remind one of the song of complaint in the musical comedy *My Fair Lady* in which the refrain is: "Why can't a woman be like me?"

Those infatuated with science are forever singing the same complaint: "Why can't philosophy be like science?"—in all those respects in which we admire the achievement of science. The answer, of course, is simply because philosophy differs remarkably from science in its mode of inquiry and in its noninvestigative method of thought. It has its own virtues, and they are different from the virtues of science.

To make this clear, I will first state the four generally acknowledged praiseworthy traits of scientific work. I will then try to explain why philosophers should never expect to emulate science in these respects, but instead should point out the quite different respects in which philosophy can claim merit for itself, and even clear superiority over science in certain accomplishments.

2

Here are the four praiseworthy traits of science.

   (i) Scientists are able to reach substantial agreement in the judgment of those regarded as competent to judge at a given time.

      a. The major disagreements in the realm of science are those between scientists at a later period and scientists at an earlier period.

      b. The resolution of these disagreements in favor of the later scientists involves steps in the advance of science from knowing less about reality to knowing more, or from knowing reality less accurately to knowing it more accurately.

  (ii) It follows from what has just been said that science can rightly claim to make progress in the course of time, and to make it more and more quickly as more individuals are engaged in scientific work.

 (iii) Science is useful in ways that enable it to claim that it showers great benefits upon human life and human society. The application of scientific knowledge in the production of technological devices to produce goods and services that are unrealizable without science is, perhaps, in many minds, the biggest feather in the hat of scientific success.

 (iv) Science has become in modern times a public enterprise; scientists cooperate with one another; they engage in teamwork; they interact. Numbers of scientists can pool their efforts in trying to solve the same problem. In this respect, scientific work stands at the opposite extreme to the painter, the composer, or the poet. The work of the individual artist is a private enterprise; rarely is this the case in science; and when it happens, it seldom remains that way.

In all of these four respects, the current attitude toward philosophy is generally negative.

(i) Philosophers at a given time do not reach agreement on the solution of problems. They do not resolve the issues on which they differ.

(ii) Philosophy does not appear to make progress from epoch to epoch, or from century to century. The retirement of philosophy in recent times to the sphere of second-order questions may have been prudent in view of the failures of philosophers to reach agreement on first-order questions, but that can hardly be regarded as progress.

(iii) Philosophy is not useful. It has no applications in technology. It bakes no bread and builds no bridges. If it is not at all useful, what good is it?

(iv) Philosophy has seldom been carried on as a public enterprise in which philosophers interact and work together as a team to solve their problems. It is much more like the individual and private work of the creative artist than it is like the pooled contributions of many scientists working together on the same problem.

3

What follows are responses to the foregoing challenges to the worth of philosophy. In my judgment these responses are quite satisfactory, though they are rarely given. They are sound because they stem from understanding the great difference between science and philosophy, a difference as great as that between mathematics and empirical science. I am going to deal with the question of progress first and then turn to the question of agreement and disagreement in philosophy.

With respect to progress in philosophy: The history of science in the West and the history of philosophy do not run parallel courses, in which empirical science advances more and more rapidly as it uses more and more powerful instruments of observation and philosophy progresses, if at all, much more slowly from epoch to epoch. One should not expect in philosophy anything like the progress that has occurred in the history of science, in view of the fact that philosophy is noninvestigative, has its empirical base in common human experience, and is continuous with common sense.

Philosophy flowered at its birth in the fifth and fourth centuries B.C. The philosophical insights and wisdom it attained in those early centuries were preserved and passed on after the Dark Ages in the mediaeval universities. The great teachers there were excellent students of Plato and Aristotle, and, as their followers, they made advances in detail, refinements in analysis, and here and there formulated new arguments for truths they received from antiquity.

Then, beginning in the seventeenth century, with the attempts by Descartes, Hobbes, Spinoza, and Locke, each trying to start philosophical thought anew, largely ignoring or rejecting the accumulated wisdom of the past, philosophy started its decline, which has continued to the present day. This decline was caused by making philosophical mistakes that could have been avoided had they been as docile students of antiquity as their predecessors in the Middle Ages.[1]

Two factors are mainly responsible for the progress that has been made in scientific knowledge. On the one hand,

---

[1] See my book *Ten Philosophical Mistakes*, especially the Epilogue, "Modern Science and Ancient Wisdom," which, I think, explains the decline of philosophical thought in modern times.

advances in observational techniques and their employment to explore new fields of phenomena result in the steady accumulation of more and more data of special experience. On the other, new theoretical insights are achieved by the development of better and more comprehensive theories. These two factors interact. The discovery of new data by investigation occasions or stimulates advances in theorizing; and new theoretical constructions often call forth experimental or investigative ingenuity in the search for supporting or refuting data. Furthermore, as we have seen, increasing specialization and ever more intensive division of labor occur in science; and this, in turn, is related to the ever-growing number of scientists at work which, in purely quantitative terms, accounts for cumulative progress at an accelerating rate.

In philosophy, there is no accumulation of new data; there are no advances in observational techniques and no new observational discoveries; there is no specialization and no division of labor. Since common experience at its core always remains the same, it does not by itself occasion or stimulate advances in theorizing. Since these things are impossible in philosophy, precisely because it is noninvestigative, it has made no progress, or less progress and at a much slower rate.

If the same kind, amount, or rate of progress could be expected of philosophy, then it would be fair to say that science is vastly superior to philosophy in making progress. It is clearly wrong, however, to expect the same kind of progress—or the same rate of progress—from a noninvestigative as from an investigative mode of inquiry, especially in view of the bearing of its investigative procedure on the main factor responsible for progress in science. To say that philosophy is inferior to science in regard to progress is like saying that a fish is inferior to a bird in locomotion. Both can move forward to an objective, each with a certain velocity, but the difference in the manner and the rate of their movement reflects the difference in the media through which they move.

What I have just said should not be interpreted as condoning philosophy's failure to make greater progress than it has so far. Common experience being a constant factor, progress in philosophy must be made on the side of theorizing rather than on the empirical side—that is, in the development of new theoretical insights, improvements in analysis, the formulation of more precise questions, the construction of more comprehensive theories, and the removal of the inconsistencies, embarrassments, paradoxes, and puzzles that have long beset philosophical thought. Some progress of this sort has been made in the past, and some has occurred quite recently, but it must nevertheless be admitted that the total extent of it falls far short of what might be reasonably expected.

In my judgment, the central reason for this lies in the fact that, for the most part, philosophical work has been carried on by thinkers working in isolation, and not as a public enterprise in which thinkers make serious efforts to cooperate with one another. A little earlier I pointed out that the ever-growing number of scientists at work accounted, in part, for accelerating, cumulative progress. The creation of departments of philosophy in our institutions of higher learning, it could be said, has greatly increased the number of philosophers at work. If this has not produced the same kind of result that the same phenomenon has produced in science—and certainly it has not—the reason, I submit, lies in the failure of the participants in the philosophical enterprise to cooperate as scientists do in their ventures.

What does this all come to? First, philosophy by its very nature cannot make the same kind and rate of progress that is made in science; to expect it to do so is to make a false demand; to denigrate philosophy for not doing so is unjustified. Second, because of the difference in the factors operative in the two disciplines, it is more difficult to make progress—and more difficult to make it steadily and at an ever-accelerating pace—in philosophy than in science.[2] Philosophy is inferior to science now not because it fails to make the same kind or rate of progress, but because it fails to advance in a way and at a pace that is as appropriate to its noninvestigative character as the manner and pace of scientific progress is appropriate to a discipline that is investigative in method. If philosophy were to do as well in its medium as science does in its, the correct statement of the case would not be that philosophy is inferior to science in progress, but only that it is distinctly different in this respect.

With respect to agreement and disagreement in philosophy: One of the most common complaints about philosophy is that philosophers always disagree. This complaint is given added force by pointing out that, in contrast to philosophy, there is a large area of agreement among scientists. Furthermore, when scientists disagree, we expect them to work at and succeed in settling their differences. They have at their disposal and they employ effective implements of decision whereby they can resolve their disagreements and obtain a concurrence of opinion among those qualified to judge the matters under dispute.

Philosophical disagreements persist; or, to speak more accurately, since there is so little genuine disagreement or joining of issues in philosophy, differences of opinion remain unclarified, undebated, and unresolved. It is frequently far from clear that philosophers who appear to differ are even addressing themselves to the same subject or trying to answer the same question.

---

[2] In the mid-nineteenth century, William Whewell, head of Trinity College, Cambridge University, and himself an eminent philosopher of science, proposed a reform in the curriculum for the undergraduate degree. One of its guiding principles was his distinction between permanent and progressive studies. In the category of permanent studies, Whewell placed portions of science and mathematics, but it mainly comprised the classics of imaginative literature and philosophy. In his view, the category of progressive studies consisted largely of science and mathematics.

This state of affairs gives rise to the widely prevalent judgment that, in this matter of agreement and disagreement, philosophy is plainly inferior to science. Nevertheless, as in the matter of progress, the comparison of science and philosophy with respect to agreement is falsely drawn and the judgment based on it is unfairly made.

One difference between science and philosophy, already pointed out, helps us to rectify the erroneous impression that agreement generally obtains in science while disagreement is rife in philosophy. Because philosophy relies solely on common experience in dealing with first-order questions, philosophers widely separated in time can be treated as contemporaries, whereas with the ever-changing state of the data acquired by ongoing investigation, only scientists working at the same time can function as contemporaries. This basic difference between science and philosophy results in a different temporal pattern of agreement and disagreement in each, to whatever extent genuine agreements and disagreements do, in fact, exist.

The scientists of a given century or time tend to disagree with and reject the formulations of earlier scientists, largely because the latter are based on insufficient data. Disagreement in science occurs vertically across the centuries; and most of the agreements in science occur along the same horizontal time line among scientists at work during the same period. By contrast, there is considerable and often unnoticed agreement across the centuries among philosophers living at different times; the striking disagreements—or differences of opinion—occur mainly among philosophers alive at the same time. In short, we find some measure of agreement and of disagreement in both science and philosophy, but we find the temporal pattern of it quite different in each case.

The judgment that philosophy is inferior to science with respect to agreement focuses entirely on the horizontal time line, where we find the maximum degree of agreement among scientists and the minimum degree of it among philosophers. If we shift our attention to the vertical time line, there is some ground for the opposite judgment. Looking at the opinions of scientists in an earlier century, we come away with the impression of substantial and extensive disagreement, whereas we find a considerable measure of agreement among philosophers across the centuries.

To judge philosophy inferior by expecting or demanding that its pattern of agreement and disagreement should conform to the pattern exhibited by science is to judge it by reference to a model or standard that is as inapplicable as the model of scientific progress is inapplicable to philosophy. To dismiss this judgment as wrongly made, however, is not to condone philosophy for its failure to achieve what might be reasonably expected of it on its own terms.

The most crucial failure of philosophy so far is the failure of philosophers to face each other in clear and genuine disagreements, to join issue and engage in the debate of disputed questions. Only when this defect is overcome will philosophers be able to settle their differences by rational means and achieve the measure of agreement that can be reasonably expected of them.

Here, as with respect to progress, the difficulties are greater for philosophy. The decision between competing scientific formulations by reference to crucial data obtained by investigation is easier than the resolution of philosophical issues by rational debate. Nevertheless, the difficulties that confront philosophy with respect to agreement and disagreement can be surmounted in the same way that the difficulties it faces with respect to progress can be overcome—namely, by the conduct of philosophy as a public, rather than a private enterprise.

When philosophy is properly conducted as a public enterprise and philosophers work cooperatively, they will succeed to a much greater extent than they do now in addressing themselves to the same problems, clearly joining issue where they differ in their answers, and carrying on rational debate of the issues in a way that holds some promise of their eventual resolution.[3]

It is, therefore, fair to say that philosophy is at present inferior to science with respect to agreement and disagreement, but *only if one means* that philosophy has not yet achieved what can reasonably be expected of it—a measure and a pattern of agreement and disagreement appropriate to its character as a noninvestigative discipline and hence distinctly different from the measure and pattern of these things in science.

I reiterate that philosophy, like science, can be conducted as a public enterprise, wherein philosophers work cooperatively. In the very nature of the case that is possible, even though little has been done to move philosophy in that direction. Nevertheless, should philosophy ever fully realize what is inherently possible, its achievement with respect to agreement and disagreement will be as commendable as the achievement of science in the same respect, for each will then have done all it can do within the limitations of its method as a mode of inquiry and appropriate to its character as a type of knowledge.

With respect to the use of philosophy: Knowledge is useful. What is known may not always be put to use in the management or conduct of human affairs or in the control of man's environment, but it always can be. If it is not, its latent usefulness remains to be exploited in the future. Intrinsically useless knowledge is a contradiction in terms.

[3] For a discussion of the propadeutic service performed for philosophy by dialectical work, which cannot be done except as a public and cooperative enterprise, see my book *The Idea of Freedom*, Vol. I, Part III, especially Chapter 8. Such work should help philosophers to agree about the issues on which they differ and to argue more relevantly with one another, thus increasing the degree to which they cooperate and interact. This was the point of Professor Arthur Lovejoy's presidential address in 1916 before the American Philosophical Association on some conditions of progress in philosophy.

We often speak of knowledge in use as applied knowledge. The Greek philosophers laid down a basic division in the use or application of knowledge, which is worth recalling. In the sphere of the practical they distinguished between *production* and *action*—between the sphere of man's efforts to make things or to control the forces of nature in order to achieve certain results, and the sphere of human conduct, both individual and social. They also distinguished between knowledge itself, as capable of being used or applied, and a special type of knowledge which they said must be added in order to put knowledge to use.

The latter—the special knowledge that is operative when knowledge is put to use—the Greeks called *technē*. The English equivalent of that word is, of course, "technique," but I prefer the more colloquial "know-how."

Distinguishing between the spheres of application or use, we can speak of productive and practical know-how—that is, the know-how that is involved in the business of making things or achieving desired effects and results and the know-how that is involved in applying knowledge to the affairs of action, the problems of individual conduct and the conduct of society.

Practical know-how, particularly that form of it which is involved in applying scientific knowledge, concerns the means for achieving whatever ends of individual or social action we set up for ourselves. It does not, and cannot, tell us what ends we ought to pursue, but it may tell us what ends are, or are not, practicable to pursue because adequate means are, or are not, available; it often gives us knowledge of the diverse means that are available for achieving a particular goal; and, with respect to alternative means, it often enables us to make a judgment about their relative efficiency or effectiveness.

Productive know-how, again especially that form of it which is involved in applying scientific knowledge, concerns the steps to be taken in making useful tools and machines, improving their efficiency, and shaping or controlling nature to serve our purposes. It does not, and cannot, tell us what our purposes ought to be; it merely helps us to realize whatever purposes we may have, so far as their realization depends upon instrumentalities that we can devise or controls that we can exercise over natural processes. Currently, such productive know-how, based on science, is called technology.[4]

4

It would be reasonable to expect each different branch of knowledge to have a kind of usefulness or application distinctively and characteristically its own. What is the usefulness of philosophical knowledge? With regard to productive know-how it is generally recognized that philosophy is totally useless; it has no technological applications whatsoever. As William James said, it "bakes no bread"; it builds no bridges, makes no bombs, invents no instruments, concocts no poisons, harnesses no power, and so forth. Francis Bacon's famous remark that knowledge is power (that is, that knowledge gives us mastery over nature and an ability to produce or control effects according to our wishes) is as false in the case of philosophical knowledge as it is true in the case of scientific knowledge.

With regard to practical know-how, philosophy is just as deficient, though this is not as generally recognized as its deficiency with regard to productive know-how. Philosophical knowledge does not instruct us concerning the means available for achieving whatever results we desire, or whatever goals or objectives we may set ourselves. By itself (without the addition of scientific knowledge), it does not tell us whether our practical purposes are or are not practicable, because there are or are not adequate means for achieving

[4]The word "technology," which, according to its Greek roots, should mean "know-that about know-how," is thus currently used as if it had the same meaning as "technique" (i.e., skill or know-how).

them. Nor does it enable us to judge the relative efficiency or effectiveness of competing means for achieving the same ends.

Is philosophy, then, totally useless? The answer must be in the affirmative if the usefulness of knowledge is exhaustively represented by the kinds of productive and practical know-how that have their basis in scientific knowledge. But that is not the whole story.

As I pointed out earlier, science does not and cannot tell us what ends we *ought* to pursue; it does not and cannot tell us what our purposes *ought* to be. However useful it is productively, it does not tell us whether we *ought* or *ought not* to produce certain things (such as thermonuclear bombs or supersonic transport planes); it does not tell us whether we *ought* or *ought not* to exercise certain controls over natural processes (such as human procreation or changes in weather). However useful it is practically, it does not tell us whether we *ought* or *ought not* to employ certain means to achieve our ends, on any basis other than their relative efficiency; it does not tell us whether one goal *ought* or *ought not* to be preferred to another. It does not tell us, in short, what we *ought* or *ought not* to do and what we *ought* or *ought not* to seek.

In Chapter 5, where I dealt with the tests of truth in philosophy, I pointed out that there were two distinct modes of truth, not one. The first is the correspondence theory of truth, according to which our thinking about reality is true if it agrees with the way things really are or are not. We called this mode of truth descriptive. It is expressed in statements that contain "is" and "is not." The other mode of truth is prescriptive, and is expressed in statements that contain the words "ought" or "ought not."

Philosophical knowledge of the first order is the dimension of philosophy in which we find descriptive truth. It is in the second dimension of philosophy that we find the prescriptive truths of ethical and political philosophy.

These truths state the categorical moral obligations that govern the conduct of our lives and the institutions of our societies. In this second dimension, we find the use that philosophy uniquely confers on us.

The difference in the usefulness of science and philosophy corresponds to the difference in their methods as modes of inquiry. No question properly belongs to science which cannot be answered or elucidated by investigation. That is precisely why no *ought* question is scientific and why, therefore, science includes no prescriptive or normative branch, no *ought* knowledge.

Beginning in the seventeenth century, the natural sciences gradually separated themselves from speculative philosophy. More recently, the social sciences have declared their independence of philosophy in its prescriptive or normative dimensions. In order to establish themselves as subdivisions of science, such disciplines as economics, politics, and sociology had to eschew all normative considerations (that is, all *ought* questions or, as they are sometimes called, questions of value). They had to become purely descriptive, in this respect exactly like the natural sciences. They had to restrict themselves to questions of how men do, in fact, behave, individually and socially, and forego all attempts to say how they ought in principle to behave.

Science and philosophy as public enterprises: There is no question that it is advantageous for each to be conducted as a public rather than a private enterprise. But the differences in their modes of inquiry and their methods make it impossible for them to be public enterprises in the same way, and also make it more difficult for philosophy than for science to be thus conducted.

If philosophy and science were as much alike as two subdivisions of science (for example, physics and chemistry or zoology and botany), the expectation of similar performance would be justified. That, however, is not the case. All the subdivisions of science involve essentially the same type of method: they are all investigative as well as empirical disciplines. Philosophy is noninvestigative. Hence, the comparability of science and philosophy as modes of inquiry that seek knowledge in the form of *doxa* must be qualified by the essential difference between an investigative and noninvestigative procedure in acquiring knowledge and testing theories or conclusions.

Three consequences follow from this essential difference. I call attention to them, not only because they help understanding the divergent characteristics of science and philosophy as comparable disciplines, but also because they enable us to modify the prevailing judgments about philosophy's inferiority to science with respect to agreement and progress. The comparison—and evaluation—of science and philosophy in these respects must be made with an eye on the difference between them and with due account taken of the implications of that difference.

Because science is investigative and philosophy is not, specialization and division of labor are possible in science as they are not in philosophy—at least not to the same extent.

The multiplicity of the major subdivisions of science, and the further subsectioning of the major subdivisions, is closely related to the multiplicity of specific techniques for carrying on the investigation of nature or society, each a technique for exploring a special field of phenomena. Men become specialists in science through mastering one or more of these techniques. No one can master all of them. The ideal of the generalist in science may, in the remote past, have had the appearance of attainability, but it does so no longer. To be a scientist now is to be a specialist in science. The total work of science is thus accomplished by the specialization of its work-

ers and by an intensive division of labor, not only on the side
of investigation, but also on the side of theoretical developments or constructions relevant to the data of investigation in
a particular field.

Turning to philosophy, we find an opposite state of affairs. The core of common experience to which the empirical
philosopher appeals is the same for all; and common or ordinary experience involves no specialized techniques. Hence,
there is and can be no basis for specialization or for division
of labor in philosophy on the empirical side. These things
naturally pertain to the work of men when they investigate,
just as naturally they play no part in the work of men when
they do not.

On the theoretical side, there is some possibility of a
division of labor in philosophy—as between logic and metaphysics, or between metaphysics and ethics. In fact, specialization has occurred both in the university teaching of
philosophy and in the concentration of this or that professor
of philosophy upon this or that sector of philosophical inquiry. Nevertheless, it remains *possible* for one man to make
contributions in all the major sectors of philosophical
thought.[5] The great philosophers of the past have certainly
been generalists in philosophy; and in our own century the
writings of Dewey, Russell, Whitehead, Bergson, Santayana,
and Maritain touch on all the major questions of philosophy.
This sufficiently makes the point of contrast between science
and philosophy, for, though in antiquity, before specialization took place, Aristotle could make contributions to the
major fields of science, that is no longer possible. In fact,
specialization and division of labor have now reached the

---

[5] It may be that under the prevailing conditions of academic life, professors of
philosophy have to become specialists in one philosophical area or another. But,
ideally, philosophers should not be specialists as scientists and mathematicians are,
but generalists, working in all of philosophy's four dimensions.

point at which it is almost impossible for one man to do outstanding theoretical work in more than a single field of scientific research.

Because there is so much specialization and division of labor in science, and so little in philosophy, as a consequence of the fact that one is and the other is not investigative, it follows as a further consequence that the authority of experts must be relied on in science and cannot be relied on in philosophy.

The individual scientist accepts the findings of other scientists—both in his own and other fields—without redoing the investigations on which those findings are based. He may, in rare instances, check the data by repeating the experiment, but for the most part, especially with regard to matters not immediately within his own special field of research, he proceeds by accepting the findings of reputable experts. He cannot do otherwise and get his own work done.

In many cases, though not in all, the individual scientist also accepts the theoretical conclusions reached by other scientists, if these have the authority of recognized experts, without checking all the steps by which those conclusions were originally reached or tested. In other words, a highly specialized scientist, working in some narrow corner of the whole scientific enterprise, accepts a large body of scientific opinions on the authority of other scientists. It would be impossible for him or her to do otherwise.

Since philosophers proceed entirely in terms of common experience to which all have equal access, and since it is by reference to common experience that philosophical theories or conclusions must be tested, philosophers need never accept a single philosophical opinion on the authority of other philosophers. On the contrary, whatever theories a philosopher holds and whatever conclusions he reaches he can and should arrive at them by judgments he himself makes in light of the very same evidence that is available to all others, including all other philosophers. Where, in the case of scientific work, the individual cannot dispense with the authority of his fellow workers, he cannot, in the case of philosophical work, rely on it. One might go further and say that the person who accepts any philosophical opinions whatsoever simply on the authority of their spokesmen, no matter how eminent, is no philosopher.

Because science depends on special experience acquired by investigation, whereas philosophy relies on and appeals only to the common experience of mankind which, at its core, is the same for all individuals at all times and places, philosophers have a contemporaneity that scientists cannot have.

Philosophical questions that arise from and relate to common experience can make contemporaries of philosophers as far apart in time and place as Plato and Bradley, Aristotle and Dewey, Augustine and William James. Another way of saying this is that there is no purely philosophical question that concerns us today to which it would be impossible to find an answer given by a philosopher who lived at some prior time. Earlier philosophers may not have actually considered all the questions with which we are concerned, but in many cases they did, and in all cases they *could* have. Hence, in dealing with controversies about philosophical matters, the disputants may be drawn from centuries far apart.

Not all philosophical questions have the timelessness just indicated. This characteristic pertains only to those purely philosophical problems that depend exclusively on common experience for their solution and involve no admixture of scientific knowledge. What I have called mixed questions in philosophy—especially those that depend, both for their formulation and solution, on the state of scientific knowledge—vary from time to time. Those that confront philosophers today are certainly not the same as those faced by Aristotle or Descartes. The same holds true of those mixed questions in philosophy which depend on special historical knowledge, and of those which lie athwart the border that separates philosophy from revealed religion.

With these exceptions noted, let me repeat the point: purely philosophical problems are of such a nature that the philosophers who tackle them *can have the character of contemporaries* despite their wide separation in time and place. The accidents of their immersion in different cultural milieus may affect their vocabularies and their notional idioms, but this does not prevent them from being construed as addressing themselves to the *same* problems and as engaging in debate concerning the merits of competing solutions.

The very opposite is the case in science. A scientific dispute usually, if not always, involves individuals living at the same time. At any time, the current scientific problems to be solved are conditioned by the state of the data currently in hand or the state of the research currently being carried forward. Competing theories are sponsored by individuals who take account of the latest findings of research and of the directions taken by investigations going on. Archimedes, Galileo, Newton, and Einstein cannot function as contemporaries in the way in which Aristotle, Aquinas, Locke, and William James can.

Let me state this point in still another way: the whole record of past philosophical thought can have critical relevance to current philosophical problems, whereas the whole record of past scientific work is not as relevant to current research and theorizing. A much larger portion of the scientific past has only antiquarian interest for scientists today. If there are philosophers today who would say that an equally large portion of the philosophical past can be similarly regarded, their view of this matter, I submit, stems from their relegation of philosophy to the plane of second-order questions, or to their not recognizing the role of common experience in the formulation and solution of first-order questions that are purely philosophical.

5

In light of all the foregoing considerations, the final question to be faced is one of evaluation. What value should we place on philosophy vis-à-vis science—in our culture, in our educational institutions, and in our lives, personally and socially?

To persuade readers that my answer to this question is correct, let me ask them to remember the four dimensions of philosophy as they are distinguished in this book. To help them do this, I am going to set forth below elaborated renditions of Parts Two and Three in the Contents.

PART THREE: The Third and Fourth Dimensions:
Second-Order Analytical Thought

With that general scheme before us of philosophy's four-dimensional domain, does it not follow that a culture, an education, and a life bereft of philosophy is a poor one, indeed, poorer by far than a culture, education, and life that is enriched by philosophy?

Does it not also follow that, of the four dimensions, only one of them is, like science and history, first-order *descriptive* knowledge of reality? If so, is not the first-order *prescriptive* knowledge to be found in ethical and political philosophy a highly desirable addition to all that we can ever learn from science and history?

That is not the only desirable addition to the knowledge we can derive from science and history, for they are limited to first-order knowledge by their investigative mode of inquiry. They are incapable of enlarging our understanding by the second-order work, or philosophical analysis, with respect to ideas and all branches of knowledge. Without the contributions made by philosophy, to be discussed in Chapters 9, 10, and 11, we would be left with voids that science and history cannot fill.

Even in the one sphere in which the contributions of science and philosophy are comparable—our knowledge of reality—philosophy, because it is noninvestigative, can answer questions that are beyond the reach of investigative science—questions that are more profound and penetrating than any questions answerable by science. By virtue of its being investigative, science is limited to the experienceable world of physical nature. Philosophical thought can extend its inquiries into transempirical reality. It is philosophy, not science, that takes the overall view.

Furthermore, when there is an apparent conflict between science and philosophy, it is to philosophy that we must turn for the resolution. Science cannot provide it. When scientists such as Einstein, Bohr, and Heisenberg become involved with mixed questions, they must philosophize. They cannot discuss these questions merely as scientists; the principles for the statement and solution of such problems come from philosophy, not from science.

For all these reasons, I think we are compelled to regard the contributions of philosophy as having greater value for us than the contributions of science. I say this even though we must all gratefully acknowledge the benefits that science and its technological applications confer upon us. The power that science gives us over our environment, health, and lives can, as we all know, be either misused and misdirected, or used with good purpose and results. Without the prescriptive knowledge given us by ethical and political philosophy, we have no guidance in the use of that power, directing it to the ends of a good life and a good society. The more power science and technology confer upon us, the more dangerous and malevolent that power may become unless its use is checked and guided by moral obligations stemming from our philosophical knowledge of how we ought to conduct our lives and our society.

PART TWO

Philosophical

Knowledge:

The First Two

Dimensions

CHAPTER 8

Regarding Philosophical
Knowledge

I

This chapter serves as a prefatory explanation of what readers can expect to find in Chapters 9 and 10; and, by way of anticipation, in Chapters 12 and 13.

We learned two things in Chapter 7 that should be reiterated and stressed here. One is that it is only with regard to descriptive knowledge of whatever there is to be known that philosophy and science appear to have the same scope and that they find themselves at issue with one another about what can be asserted as true or false. Therefore, it is only in Chapter 9 that we are still concerned to draw a line between the questions science is competent to answer and the questions that are only for philosophy.

To repeat Wittgenstein's famous dictum, "whereof one cannot speak, thereof one should be silent," I am saying that the sciences—and scientists—should be silent about all the questions that are totally beyond their powers to answer, not only the questions raised in moral and political philosophy, as well as all the matters pertaining to philosophical analysis, but also all matters in the sphere of descriptive knowledge that go beyond the scope of what can be empirically investigated and measured.

The last point should be stressed here. The extraordinary advances in investigative physics and biology in the twentieth century have tended to give scientists the false impression that they are approaching the point where whatever can be truthfully asserted about reality is within their grasp and that there is no room left for philosophy to add anything. In earlier centuries, philosophy may have had room to speculate about matters not yet investigated by science. But beginning in modern times, and increasingly in the nineteenth and twentieth centuries, what were hitherto matters for philosophical speculation have been taken over by scientific investigation. What was merely problematic before has become established as empirical knowledge.

This, in fact, is the positivist claim of Auguste Comte. Most scientists today are positivists, claiming, along with Comte, that all valid descriptive knowledge of reality belongs to science. In the course of centuries, we have made the steps of progress that Comte predicted. We at last recognize that what in earlier centuries was regarded as religious knowledge consisted of myths and superstitions. We have gone beyond the era of philosophy as well as of religion, and the knowledge claimed by philosophers is now seen to be merely unfounded speculation on their part. As Auguste Comte tells the history of mankind, it consists of three epochs—the epoch of religion, the epoch of philosophy, and the epoch of the positive science, in which we at last have achieved genuine knowledge of all that can be known about reality.

The dogmatic claims of positivism are widely prevalent at the end of the twentieth century, not only among scientists, but also among all those who have been miseducated in our colleges and universities, as well as in the unthinking multitudes who are overly impressed by the achievements of science and technology.

It is the central thesis of this book that such positivism is a mistake. There are transempirical aspects of reality that cannot be scientifically investigated and measured. Stephen Hawking is egregiously in error when he asserts that what cannot be investigated and measured by physicists does not exist in reality.

In addition, there is knowledge of reality through common experience and common sense that falls outside the sphere of the special experience that scientific investigation relies upon for the knowledge it acquires.

2

The traditional name for descriptive philosophical knowledge is metaphysics, as the traditional names for prescriptive knowledge are moral and political philosophy.

I am going to use the term "metaphysics" to cover a range of philosophical inquiries: the philosophy of nature (or philosophical physics), the philosophy of mind (or philosophical psychology),[1] and philosophical theology, which is the high point of metaphysics. If the line that separates questions about the knowledge that can and cannot be answered by investigative scientific procedures were clearly understood, scientists would never challenge the descriptive knowledge of reality propounded by philosophy. But when this is not the case, illegitimate confrontations and controversies arise. This is true even with respect to philosophical theology, a field regarding which scientific cosmologists should be aware of their ignorance or innocence and welcome the instruction they need from philosophy.

In the ancient and mediaeval epochs of philosophy, the stated scope of metaphysics would have been different. Aristotle, for example, would have distinguished it from physics and mathematics, and defined it as knowledge of being *qua*

---

[1] The empirical science of psychology is a behavorial science, as is animal psychology. It gives us no knowledge of human nature, of the kind we get from philosophical psychology.

being and the modes of being. The great metaphysical treatise of Thomas Aquinas was entitled *De Ente et Essentia (On Being and Essence)*. In the early decades of the twentieth century, such Thomist philosophers as Etienne Gilson and Jacques Maritain wrote books that can be consulted for expositions of traditional metaphysics.[2]

An exposition of metaphysical knowledge in the latter half of the twentieth century—especially one that is intended for everyone's understanding—must diverge from the traditional Aristotelian and Thomistic exposition, while still retaining some of its basic insights and principles. Let me explain why.

Until modern times there were no denials of a knowable reality, except by extreme skeptics who challenged the attainment of truth in science as well as in philosophy. Until modern times no philosopher, certainly none of any eminence, was an idealist, denying the existence of a reality independent of the human mind, a reality that is what it is whether human beings think about it or not and regardless of how they think about it. Until modern times there were no attempts to prove the existence of an external world and there was no problem of a discrepancy between appearance and reality.[3]

These extraordinary developments in modern thought are attributable to a series of basic philosophical mistakes, among which two are crucially consequential. One is the error of

[2] Etienne Gilson, *Being and Some Philosophers* (Toronto: Pontifical Institute of Mediaeval Studies, 1949) and *God and Philosophy* (New Haven: Yale University Press, 1941); Jacques Maritain, *A Preface to Metaphysics: Seven Lectures on Being* (New York: Sheed & Ward, 1939).

[3] It should be said here that most of the great scientists of the modern era have never succumbed to idealism. They do not doubt or deny the existence of an independent reality. It is the object of their study. In the field of cosmology and evolutionary biology, they assert the existence of cosmic realities and geological epochs before human beings existed on earth, so humans cannot be charged with regarding an independent reality as a figment of their minds.

supposing that the direct and immediate objects of our minds are our own sensations and perceptions, imaginations, and memories and concepts (for which the word "ideas" is misused), instead of recognizing that what we miscall our ideas are *that by which* we apprehend whatever we apprehend instead of being *that which* we apprehend. Ideas must, therefore, be regarded as representations of a reality that cannot be directly and immediately apprehended.

The second crucial error is the denial of the intellect as a separate cognitive power or faculty, dependent to some extent on all the sensitive faculties, but competent to deal with aspects of reality that are beyond the reach of the senses. If it were true that all our cognitive apparatus consisted of the exterior and the interior senses, including memory and imagination, then it would also be true that the empirical sciences give us all the descriptive knowledge of reality that we can attain.

If these two errors had not been made in modern times, the history of modern thought would not be filled with all its epistemological puzzles, and twentieth-century thought would not be plagued by all the mistakes it has made about language and meaning.

Lest readers suppose that I am exaggerating the plight of philosophy at the end of the twentieth century, I would like to quote at length from an article by Professor Gertrude Himmelfarb of the City University of New York entitled "The Abyss Revisited" which appeared in *The American Scholar* in Summer 1992. After dealing with the abyss of deconstructionism, fomented by Jacques Derrida and Paul de Man, Professor Himmelfarb turns our attention to the abyss in philosophy, which is the denial of reality and truth. She writes:

> Philosophy also has its abysses, and some philosophers are confronting them in the same way—playfully and irreverently. Richard Rorty, currently one of America's most respected phi-

losophers, calls himself a pragmatist, but in so "light-minded" a fashion that one can hardly recognize any kinship with his notably grave progenitor, John Dewey.

The main principle governing Rorty's philosophy is that there is no fixed or fundamental principle, no "essential" truth or reality. Indeed, philosophy, he says, no longer exists as an independent discipline. Marx once promised to abolish philosophy by replacing it with "positive science" (that is, Marxism), which he deemed to be scientific rather than philosophical because it was simply the depiction of "reality." Rorty promises to abolish philosophy by abolishing reality itself, which he regards as the arbitrary construct of the philosopher. Unlike Marx, he believes that his revolution is already largely accomplished. It is getting more and more difficult, he good-humoredly observes, to locate "a real live metaphysical prig," who thinks there is a reality to be examined and a truth about reality to be discovered. There are a few such dodoes left, to be sure. "You can still find philosophy professors who will solemnly tell you that they are seeking *the truth,* not just a story or a consensus but an honest-to-God, down-home, accurate representation of the way the world is. A few of them will even claim to write in a clear, precise, transparent way, priding themselves on manly straightforwardness, or abjuring 'literary' devices." Rorty himself, happily, has given up any such obsolete "philosophical machismo." He has even gone so far in repudiating "machismo" as to use the feminine pronoun in referring to the "anti-essentialist" philosopher and the masculine pronoun to the "essentialist"—this after identifying himself as an "anti-essentialist."

Rather than seek an essential truth, philosophers should choose to "dream up as many new contexts as possible . . . to be as polymorphous in our adjustments as possible, to recontextualize for the hell of it." They should, in fact, become philosophers-cum-poets, adopting a "light-minded aestheticism" to traditional philosophical questions, for only such an aestheticism can further the "disenchantment of the world." This disenchantment, moreover, must extend itself to morality as well as truth. Just because other people take moral issues seriously does not mean that one should share that seriousness. On the contrary, one should "josh them" out of the habit of being serious and get them to look at moral issues aesthetically, playfully.

The problem with "taking philosophy seriously," Rorty explains, is that to do so is not only philosophically naive, positing a reality and a truth that do not exist, but politically dangerous, since essentialism encourages fundamentalism and fanaticism of the kind displayed by Shiites, Marxists, and Nazis. This is Heidegger's great fault. It is not his particular doctrines about the nature of man, reason, or history that are "intrinsically fascistic." Nor are his doctrines invalidated by the fact that he himself was a Nazi, an anti-Semite, and altogether "a rather nasty peice of work." His mistake was rather in thinking that "philosophy must be taken seriously." Rorty warns us against the same mistake. An original philosopher is the product of a "neural kink," and one should no more look to him for wisdom or morality than to an original mathematician, or microbiologist, or chess master. Heidegger is original in this sense, and one should take from him and make of him what one likes—which is not at all, Rorty admits, what Heidegger might have liked. The proper approach to Heidegger is "to read his books as he would not have wished them to be read: in a cool hour, with curiosity, and an open, tolerant mind."

Heidegger looked into the abyss of philosophy and saw the beasts of Nazism—became, in fact, a Nazi. Rorty looks into the abyss of Heidegger—coolly, curiously, tolerantly—and sees not Heidegger as he saw himself, indeed as he was, but an "original and interesting writer." Divorced from the essential truth, the practical morality, and the political consequences of his own philosophy, Heidegger can be readily assimilated into Rorty's philosophy. By the same token, we can look into Rorty and see him not as he sees himself, as the only reliable philosopher of liberal democracy, but as the proponent of a relativism so extreme as to verge on nihilism—a nihilism that may subvert liberal democracy together with all the other priggish metaphysical notions about truth, morality, and reality.[4]

I have dealt with these modern errors, especially the error that leads to modern idealism and the error that calls for a proof of the existence of the external world, in *Intellect: Mind Over Matter*. See Part Two, entitled "Serious Mistakes," particularly Chapters 7 and 8. For my critique of Richard Rorty and others like him, such as Nelson Goodman and Jerome Bruner, see pages 104–105.[5]

3

The modern errors that influenced Kant and led him to formulate his Copernican revolution in philosophy started with Descartes and Hobbes, Locke, and especially Hume. It was Kant's reaction to them that produced his *Prolegomena to Any Future Metaphysic* and *Critique of Pure Reason*.

What Kant called a Copernican revolution in philosophy was aptly named. It was like replacing the Ptolemaic earth-centered astronomy with the sun revolving around the earth by the Copernican sun-centered astronomy with the earth revolving around the sun. Kant's revolution in philosophy had the human mind constituting all possible experience instead of having experience based on a reality that is independent of the human mind.

Kant did not deny the existence of an independent reality, but for him it—the *Ding an sich*, the thing in itself—was unknowable. The human mind was not a *tabula rasa* before our sensitive acquaintance with the external world generated our perceptual knowledge of reality and our intellectual

---

[4] Gertrude Himmelfarb, "The Abyss Revisited," in *The American Scholar*, Vol. 61, No. 3, Summer 1992, pp. 343-45. Reprinted by permission from *The American Scholar*. Copyright © 1992 by the author.

[5] I also recommend examining Chapters 1 through 4 in my book *Ten Philosophical Mistakes*.

power enabled us to form concepts that gave us an understanding of it. Instead, the human mind had innate—Kant called them transcendental—forms of intuition of space and time and innate or transcendental categories of understanding. These constituted our experience, beyond which we could not go without falling into error.

It certainly was a revolution to go from regarding an independent reality as that which was to be known and could be known to dismissing it as totally beyond our ken. Kant's aim was to give certainty to the judgments made in Newtonian physics and Euclidean geometry which, if Hume's erroneous psychology went uncorrected, remained in the realm of doubt. But instead of correcting Hume's errors, Kant concocted an elaborate machinery, as phony as it was ingenious, for establishing Newton's physics with a certitude that we now know it did not have, and for making Euclid's geometry the only geometry, which we know now it never was.

The traditional definition of truth from Plato and Aristotle on was that truth in the human mind consisted in its being in conformity with an independent reality. Kant outlawed such truth by denying a knowable independent reality with which the mind could conform. In place of it was the certitude of the judgments made by the mind about an experience constituted by the mind's own transcendental forms and categories. The ground of certitude in both science and philosophy came from the structure of the human mind, not from the structure of reality.

All the subsequent forms of idealism in the nineteenth and twentieth centuries stemmed from Kant, not only the Hegelian objective idealism that invented an absolute mind as the all-encompassing reality, but also the pluralistic idealisms to be found in the writings of Rorty, Goodman, and Bruner. What is common to all of them is the denial of an independent reality and of truth as the mind's conformity to it. Of course, if knowledge consists in true judgments about reality, this undercuts knowledge in science as well as in philosophy.

Kant did not deny the existence of a reality independent of the human mind. But he regarded it as unknowable and, therefore, useless in relation to all our cognitive aspirations. The next step inevitably followed: to deny the existence of something as useless as an unknowable reality.

4

The problem of appearance and reality takes many forms, all of them involving some discrepancies between the way things really are and the way they appear to us. For our present purposes, I wish to discuss two aspects of this problem.

The first arises with respect to our perceptual judgments. It must first be understood that only in perception is our apprehension of the perceived object inseparable from the judgment that the object exists in reality. This does not occur in the apprehension of any other objects—objects of memory or imagination, or of conceptual thought.

In all of these cases, there is no coincidental existential judgment. We must always ask whether or not the apprehended object also exists now in reality, or did once exist, or perhaps will exist in the future. It is only in perception that we cannot say that we perceive something and also ask whether that which we perceive exists in reality. If we perceive it, it does exist in reality. If it does not exist, then we are hallucinating, not perceiving.

I have discussed this matter more fully in *Some Questions About Language.*[6] In that context I considered the possibility of a discrepancy between appearance and reality—between the way a perceptible thing existing in reality differs from

[6] See *Some Questions About Language: A Theory of Human Discourse and Its Objects* (La Salle, Ill.: Open Court Publishing Co., 1976; First Paperback Edition, 1991), pp. 117–18. See also *Intellect: Mind Over Matter*, p. 112.

how it appears to us when it is a perceptual object, not a perceptible thing.

How is the perceptual object related to the really existing thing which causes our perception of that object?

The question applies only to the object of perception, and not to any other objects of apprehension—objects of memory, imagination, and thought. It is only in the case of perception that we have the pervasive and almost incorrigible impression that what we are perceiving is a really existent thing and not an object having intentional existence. Only in this one type of apprehension, do we apply the distinction between the apprehensible and the apprehended: we speak of things that we are not now perceiving as perceptible, and this leads us to speak of things as perceived when the perception of them occurs. We then tend to identify the thing-as-perceived with the perceptual object, though the thing, either as perceptible or as perceived, exists in reality and the perceptual object exists only intentionally. The sharp distinction between things and objects seems to vanish in the case of perception, and with it also the equally sharp distinction between apprehending and knowing; for if in perception we are apprehending things, not just objects, then perception would appear to be an act of judgment involving, at least implicitly, an existential assertion. . . .

Let me begin by facing the question exactly in the terms in which it has been posed. It asks about the relationship between the perceptual object and the perceptible thing which, when it acts in an appropriate way upon our sense-organs, causes us to perceive it. There would appear to be only the following alternative answers to that question: either (i) the perceptible thing and the perceptual object are identical, i.e., they are one in every respect; or (ii) they are nonidentical, i.e., the perceptible thing and the perceptual object are two distinct entities, each having its own mode of existence. Adopting either horn of this dilemma leads to unsatisfactory consequences.

If the perceptible thing were in every respect identical with the perceptual object, then the perceptible physical thing would not exist when it is not perceived as an object. The perceptual object, we know, exists only as a result of the act of perception; hence when we are not perceiving, there is no perceptual object. If the perceptible thing were identical with the perceptual object, it would necessarily follow, then, that when we are not perceiving, there is no perceptible thing. We know this to be false with as much assurance as we know it to be true that when we are not perceiving there is no perceptual object. We are, therefore, compelled to conclude that the perceptible thing cannot be in every respect identical with the perceptual object.

The other alternative is equally unsatisfactory. If the perceptible thing and the perceptual object are two distinct entities, each having its own mode of existence (the one, real; the other, intentional), one of them could cease to exist while the other continues to exist. The perceptible thing that we think we are perceiving could cease to exist while, at the same time, the perceptual object continues in existence. The converse might also be the case: we could be actually perceiving the perceptible thing while, at the same time, the perceptual object might cease to exist. We cannot accept either of these diremptions between the perceptible thing and the perceptual object, diremptions which necessarily follow from the supposition that the perceptible thing and the perceptual object are two distinct entities, each having its own mode of existence.

As against the supposition that the perceptible thing and the perceptual object are completely identical, we know that perceptible physical things exist independently of their being perceived. They exist and are perceptible whether or not they are actually perceived. As against the supposition that the perceptible thing and the perceptual object are two entities, each having existence independent of the other, we know that the existence of the one (the perceptual object) depends on the existence of the other (the perceptible thing). Perceptual objects do not exist unless perceptible things are being actually perceived. We know, therefore, that the perceptible thing and the perceptual object cannot be completely identical, nor can they be completely distinct. What middle ground can there be between (i) complete identity and (ii) the nonidentity of two entities each of which can exist without the other? The solution of our problem would seem to lie in the answer to that question, if one is available.

Let me state the answer first and then try to explain it. Although the perceptible thing and the perceptual object are not completely identical they are sufficiently identical to be one entity having two modes of existence. If this were true, it would also be true to say that the perceptible thing can exist even when the perceptual object does not exist, but that the perceptual object cannot exist when the perceptible thing does not exist. We observe a certain asymmetry here in the relationship of perceptible thing and perceptual object, but it is precisely such asymmetry that accords with the facts as we know them, facts that are incompatible with both of the two suppositions that we found it necessary to reject.

To explain what has just been said, I must show that there can be a relationship that lies between complete identity and nonidentity—a degree of identity which, though incomplete, is nevertheless sufficient to preclude nonidentity. The explanation is as follows:

Two things, or, to be more precise, two aspects of one thing, are existentially inseparable in a symmetrical manner if neither can exist without the other, as is the case with the two faces of a coin. Though the two faces of a coin are aspects of it which are analytically distinct as heads and tails, they are existentially inseparable.

One and the same entity may have analytically distinguishable aspects (in this case, two modes of being) which are existentially inseparable, but only in an asymmetrical, not in a symmetrical, manner. In the case of the two faces of a coin, neither can exist without the other; hence their existential inseparability is symmetrical. The inseparability is asymmetrical rather than symmetrical, however, when what we are considering is one and the same entity with two modes of being—real existence as a perceptible physical thing and intentional existence as a perceptual object. On the one hand, since the entity can have real existence as a perceptible physical thing without being actually perceived, it can have real existence without also having intentional existence as a perceptual object. On the other hand, the entity cannot have intentional existence as a perceptual object unless it also has real existence as a perceptible physical thing. Its intentional existence is inseparable from its real existence, whereas its real existence is not inseparable from its intentional existence. This is just another way of saying that these two modes of being of one and the same entity are existentially inseparable in an asymmetrical manner.

Can we say anything more about the relationship of the perceptible thing and the perceptual object, to explain further what is involved in the partial yet sufficient identity of the two? In addition to their being one entity with two modes of existence which are inseparable in an asymmetrical manner, they also stand in a one-one relationship in a large number of respects, but not in all respects. Again we must recognize a partial, yet sufficient, identity of the two.

Consider a movable and perceptible thing and two observers of it, for whom it is one and the same perceptual object. A movement of the thing from here to there will be accompanied by a perceived movement of the perceptual object from one perceived place to another. If one of two observers were to pick up a stone and throw it over his left shoulder, and if he were then to ask his associate whether he observed the flight of the stone, only to receive a reply in the negative, the person who threw the stone would know that the movable and perceptible thing was not one-one with a perceptual object which was common to his associate and himself. An affirmative answer, on the other hand, would indicate a one-one relationship between the perceptible thing and a perceptual object, which was the same object for two observers.

There can, of course, be unobservable or imperceptible changes in a physical thing, to which there will be no corresponding changes in the perceptual object. The converse would not seem to be true. Changes in the perceptual object will always correspond to changes in the perceptible thing or in the conditions of observation under which the perceptible thing is being observed. The one-one relationship is thus seen to be both asymmetrical and also partial. Nevertheless, there is a correspondence between the perceptible thing and the perceptual object in all those respects in which changes in the physical thing are perceptible; and this, together with the point previously made about the asymmetrical inseparability of the perceptible thing and the perceptual object, provides a basis for saying that they are sufficiently identical to be one entity having two modes of being—real existence, on the one hand, and intentional existence, on the other. In other words, one and the same entity is both a perceptible thing and an apprehended object, yet in such a way that its existence as a perceptible thing does not depend on its existence as an apprehended object. . . .[7]

5

The second apparent discrepancy between appearance and reality is brought to our attention by the great physicist Sir Arthur S. Eddington in the introduction to his book *The Nature of the Physical World*. He calls our attention to the fact that the table of our ordinary perceptual experience, or for that matter any other physical body—his pen or his body—is far different in its physical form from what it appears to be as we perceive it. He calls the table at which he is sitting and writing the table of ordinary experience, the kind of solid substantial thing with which all of us are familiar. The other table he calls the scientific table, the table in which there is much empty space and molecules moving about at high velocities. Let me quote his opening paragraphs:

> I have settled down to the task of writing these lectures and have drawn up my chairs to my two tables. Two tables! Yes;

[7] *Some Questions About Language*, pp. 111–15.

there are duplicates of every object about me—two tables, two chairs, two pens.

This is not a very profound beginning to a course which ought to reach transcendent levels of scientific philosophy. But we cannot touch bedrock immediately; we must scratch a bit at the surface of things first. And whenever I begin to scratch the first thing I strike is—my two tables.

One of them has been familiar to me from earliest years. It is a commonplace object of that environment which I call the world. How shall I describe it? It has extension; it is comparatively permanent; it is coloured; above all it is *substantial*. By substantial I do not merely mean that it does not collapse when I lean upon it; I mean that it is constituted of "substance" and by that word I am trying to convey to you some conception of its intrinsic nature. It is a *thing;* not like space, which is a mere negation; nor like time, which is—Heaven knows what! But that will not help you to my meaning because it is the distinctive characteristic of a "thing" to have this substantiality, and I do not think substantiality can be described better than by saying that it is the kind of nature exemplified by an ordinary table. And so we go round in circles. After all if you are a plain commonsense man, not too much worried with scientific scruples, you will be confident that you understand the nature of an ordinary table. I have even heard of plain men who had the idea that they could better understand the mystery of their own nature if scientists would discover a way of explaining it in terms of the easily comprehensible nature of a table.

Table No. 2 is my scientific table. It is a more recent acquaintance and I do not feel so familiar with it. It does not belong to the world previously mentioned—that world which spontaneously appears around me when I open my eyes, though how much of it is objective and how much subjective I do not here consider. It is part of a world which in more devious ways has forced itself on my attention. My scientific table is mostly emptiness. Sparsely scattered in that emptiness are numerous electric charges rushing about with great speed; but their combined bulk amounts to less than a billionth of the bulk of the table itself. Notwithstanding its strange construction it turns out to be an entirely efficient table. It supports my writing paper as satisfactorily as Table No. 1; for when I lay the paper on it the little electric particles with their headlong speed keep on hitting the underside, so that the paper is maintained in shuttlecock fashion at a nearly steady level. If I lean upon this table I shall not go through; or, to be strictly accurate, the chance of my scientific elbow going through my scientific table is so excessively small that it can be neglected in practical life. Reviewing their properties one by one, there seems to be nothing to choose between the two tables for ordinary purposes; but when abnormal circumstances befall, then my scientific table shows to advantage. If the house catches fire my scientific table will dissolve quite naturally into scientific smoke, whereas my familiar table undergoes a metamorphosis of its substantial nature which I can only regard as miraculous.

There is nothing *substantial* about my second table. It is nearly all empty space—space pervaded, it is true, by fields of force, but these are assigned to the category of "influences," not of "things." Even in the minute part which is not empty we must not transfer the old notion of substance. In dissecting matter into electric charges we have traveled far from that picture of it which first gave rise to the conception of substance, and the meaning of that conception—if it ever had any—has been lost by the way. The whole trend of modern scientific views is to break down the separate categories of "things," "influences," "forms," etc., and to substitute a common background of all experience. Whether we are studying a material object, a magnetic field, a geometrical figure, or a duration of time, our scientific information is summed up in measures; neither the apparatus of measurement nor the mode of using it suggests that there is anything essentially different in these problems. The measures themselves afford no ground for a classification by categories. We feel it necessary to concede some background to the measures—an external world; but the attributes of this world, except insofar as they are reflected in the measures, are outside scientific scrutiny. Science has at last revolted against attaching the exact knowledge contained in these measurements to a traditional picture-gallery of conceptions which convey no authentic information of the background and obtrude irrelevancies into the scheme of knowledge.

I will not here stress further the non-substantiality of electrons, since it is scarcely necessary to the present line of thought. Conceive them as substantially as you will, there is a vast difference between my scientific table with its substance (if any) thinly scattered in specks in a region mostly empty and the table of everyday conception which we regard as the type of solid reality—an incarnate protest against Berkeleian subjectivism. It makes all the difference in the world whether the paper before me is poised as it were on a swarm of flies and sustained in shuttlecock fashion by a series of tiny blows from the swarm underneath, or whether it is supported because there is substance below it, it being the intrinsic nature of substance to occupy space to the exclusion of other substance; all the difference in conception at least, but no difference to my practical task of writing on the paper.

I need not tell you that modern physics has by delicate test and remorseless logic assured me that my second scientific table is the only one which is really there—wherever "there" may be. On the other hand I need not tell you that modern physics will never succeed in exorcising that first table—strange compound of external nature, mental imagery, and inherited prejudice—which lies visible to my eyes and tangible to my grasp. We must bid good-bye to it for the present for we are about to turn from the familiar world to the scientific world revealed by physics. This is, or is intended to be, a wholly external world.

"You speak paradoxically of two worlds. Are they not really two aspects or two interpretations of one and the same world?"

Yes, no doubt they are ultimately to be identified after some fashion. But the process by which the external world of physics is transformed into a world of familiar acquaintance in human consciousness is outside the scope of physics. And so the world studied according to the methods of physics remains detached from the world familiar to consciousness, until after the physicist has finished his labours upon it. Provisionally, therefore, we regard the table which is the subject of physical research as altogether separate from the familiar table, without prejudging the question of their ultimate indentification. It is true that the whole scientific inquiry starts from the familiar world and in the end it must return to the familiar world; but the part of the journey over which the physicist has charge is in foreign territory.[8]

I persuaded my friend and colleague Sir Brian Pippard, who is himself an eminent British physicist and until recently head of the Cavendish Laboratory at the University of Cambridge, to comment on Eddington's two tables. He wrote:

Why only two? Surely there are at least three tables, and probably more. Let us define them before discussing how they relate to each other.

Table 1 (T_1) is the table which we say we see and talk about with others, confident that they will understand. It is the table of the marketplace whose existence is taken for granted in the ordinary course of life. We do not doubt it continues to exist when we are not present, for others who remain describe it in the same terms as we ourselves employ. To the naive realist (who has a place in the minds of us all) it is the real table, and there's no more to be said.

Table 2 (T_2) is my mental picture (or model) of a particular table, whether in view or remembered, or even imagined in a form unlike any I have ever seen.* It is my personal table, in the sense that no one else can get into my mind to know it as I know it; and I cannot know your mental picture either. Yet when you try to describe it I recognise that your picture and mine are not dissimilar; that is why we agree about the real existence of T_1, being something apart from ourselves which we each perceive

[8] Sir Arthur S. Eddington, *The Nature of the Physical World*, (New York: Macmillan and Cambridge University Press), Introduction, pp. 9–13. Copyright © 1928 by The Macmillan Company. Reprinted with permission of Cambridge University Press. Also reprinted in *The Great Ideas Today*, 1990 (Chicago: Encyclopaedia Britannica, Inc.), pp. 307–10.

* For my argument I do not need to distinguish between the mental pictures of an object in sight and of the same object remembered. It is enough that neither is T_1.

and interpret in similar ways. It is easy to conclude that T_2 is little more than a photographic image of T_1, but this is an error, if for no other reason than that the mental picture has a three-dimensional quality absent from its source material, the two-dimensional optical images thrown on the retina. Indeed, what persists in my memory is so clearly a three-dimensional table that if I walk into the room at night I can visualise its form and position well enough to stretch out my hand without hesitation to touch it.

That this mental picture is something I have constructed with marvellous, if unconscious, cunning is brought home by the experience of handling a previously unseen object in a dark room. Out of the complex sequence of pressure-sensations conveyed to my brain emerges a visual image—though until now I have never seen the object, yet I recognise it as a three-dimensional object as soon as the light is switched on.

Table 2 is the table most immediately known to me, the existence of T_1 being an inference. When a physical scientist talks about a table he is, at least initially, referring to T_1, for he is himself a creature of the marketplace, concerned only with matters he can discuss with others. He regards himself as an observer, aloof from the object of his observation, having found by experience that its behaviour is not affected by what he thinks of it.

Table 3 (T_3) is what the physicist makes of T_1 after prolonged experimentation and analysis—the table that Eddington as a physicist describes in terms of empty space and rapidly moving particles, none of which he perceives by means of sight or touch. Just as Eddington, as an ordinary man, can assert that the table he sees, touches, and is even leaning on when he delivers his lecture is a really existent table, not a fantasy of the mind, so Eddington, the theoretical physicist, has scientific grounds for asserting that the table of which he gives a scientific description also exists in reality in the same place that is occupied by the table of his perceptual experience, the table of the marketplace.

Table 4 (T_4) is something we are not ready for at present, but if it exists at all it is the table-as-it-is-in-itself, when it is neither perceived by us, nor remembered by us, nor thought about scientifically by us—the table that somehow underlies all the others. We are conscious of Tables 1, 2, and 3 in different ways—by sense perception, by memory or imagination, and by scientific thought—but, of these three tables, one, T_2, exists *only* in our minds. To T_1, T_3, and T_4 we attribute existence in reality, and we are compelled to wonder whether the table-in-itself (T_4) has the same character as the table we perceive (T_1) or the table scientifically described (T_3). Or is it something quite other, outside the range of our thought?

I shall be talking about more things than tables and shall use the symbol T to refer, as convenient, to a table or a lump of tungsten or anything else of a material nature that enters the argument. I am not sure that I understand what Eddington means by his first table, but it is T_1 alone or a combination of T_1 and T_2; his second table is T_3. My argument leads off with T_1 and T_3, the object we all recognise and what the physicist says it's made of.

It might be thought T_3 is no more than a microscopic view of T_1. For example, when a crystal of tungsten is examined by X rays, their reflection into various directions is exactly what would be expected from something composed of an orderly arrangement of identical tungsten atoms. And when we magnify the bumps on its surface a hundred million times in a field-ion microscope, the pattern we see reproduces the same arrangement of atoms. There are many other analytical tools, and the information they give dovetails so beautifully that no physicist doubts the atoms are as real as the object they constitute.

Of course, the physicist is not bound to keep in mind, at all times, this atomic picture of matter. Long before the existence of atoms was generally accepted physicists were saying useful things about matter, treating it as a T_1 rather than a T_3. A lump of tungsten is heavy, and that may be all we need to know about it; and it is hard, but we may not care how this arises from the strong preference of the atoms to pack in a particular way. The atomic theorist explains how Eddington's empty space, with a

good few particles running around, gives rise to the rigid structure, but the engineer making tungsten wire for a light bulb has
little concern for any but the gross (or macroscopic) properties,
the subject matter of classical, pre-atomic physics. Even when it
becomes necessary to consider atomic constitution it is surpris-
ing how often the chemist's and crystallographer's model kit of
balls and rods provides as much as is needed.

If only we had been able to halt scientific advance at this
point we might have continued to accept the naive realism that
controls our daily lives—a table may indeed be composed of
atoms like little hard spheres, but what we see standing there,
and remember in our mind's eye, is the real table, no more and
no less. Eddington wrote his Gifford Lectures less than a year
after the revolutionary theories of Werner Heisenberg and Er-
win Schrödinger had put paid to [destroyed] this illusion, and
one must marvel at his assimilation of the implications for physics and philosophy. In brief, we are now aware that protons and
electrons, and other atomic constituents, are not a bit like little
bullets. When they come together in an atom, and atoms come
together in molecules or larger aggregates, the individual pecu-
liarities tend to be ironed out. But they are still there, ready to
reveal themselves in the right circumstances; the operation of
lasers, and the strange properties of superconductors and su-
perfluid helium, cannot be understood without accepting that
the rules governing microscopic objects also apply to systems of
macroscopic scale, the scale of everyday perception. The paradoxes of subatomic physics refuse to be confined to their microscopic bounds. It is odd, to be sure, that one can never
discover the path by which an electron got from A to B, and
that when one knows it has left A one cannot say whether it will
or will not arrive at B, only how likely that event is. But it is
more than odd, it is distinctly disquieting to be told that a
similar indeterminacy afflicts objects and events that we are
accustomed to think are inexorably regulated by natural law.[9]

[9] Sir Brian Pippard, "Eddington's Two Tables," in *The Great Ideas Today, 1990,*
pp. 311–13. Reprinted with permission from *The Great Ideas Today, 1990.* © 1990
by Encyclopaedia Britannica, Inc.

My solution to Eddington's problem of the discrepancy between the reality of physical things and the way they appear in our perceptual experience of them differs from that proposed by Sir Brian Pippard. I am going to report my solution here by quoting what I wrote about reality and appearances in the symposium that Sir Brian and I published in *The Great Ideas Today, 1990*.

The commonsense picture of the world in which we live would appear to be shattered by what we are told by the physical scientists of our own day.

I will never forget my shock when, more than fifty years ago, I read Sir Arthur Eddington's Gifford Lectures, *The Nature of the Physical World*. In his opening remarks, Sir Arthur told his audience that the table in front of which he was standing, the table which seemed so solid to them that they would bruise their fists if they tried to punch through it, was in reality an area of largely empty space in which tiny invisible bodies were moving about at great speeds, interacting with one another in a variety of ways, and making the table appear to us to be solid, of a certain size, shape, and weight, and having certain other sensible qualities, such as its color, its smoothness, and so on.

Appearance and reality! As Sir Arthur spoke, there seemed to be no doubt in his mind which was which. The table the lecturer and his audience perceived through their eyes and could touch with their hands might appear to them to be an individual thing that had an enduring identifiable identity which could undergo change while remaining one and the same thing. That was the appearance, an appearance that might even be called illusory in comparison to the invisible and untouchable reality of the atomic particles in motion that filled the space occupied by the visible table, a space largely empty even though impenetrable by us.

My initial shock increased when I passed from thinking about the table to thinking about myself and other human beings. We were not different from the table. We, too, were individual physical things. We might appear to ourselves and to each other to be as solid as the table, perhaps somewhat softer to the touch, but just as impenetrable to a probing finger. But, in reality, the space our apparently solid bodies occupied was just as empty as that of the table. Whatever attributes or characteristics our bodies appear to have as we perceive them through our senses, they have as a result of the motions and interactions of particles that themselves had none of these sensible characteristics.

(According to this view, the imperceptible particles that compose all the objects of our ordinary perceptual experience possess only quantitative properties, no sensible qualities at all. The latter, it is maintained, exist only in our consciousness of the objects we perceive, not in the objects themselves. They have no status in reality. Thus arises the riddle about what came to be called "secondary qualities," a puzzlement that always accompanies the reductionist fallacy to which atomists are prone.)

What becomes of my personal identity, or yours, and with it moral responsibility for our actions, if each of us ceases to be one individual thing, but becomes instead a congeries of physical particles that do not remain the same particles during the span of our lifetime?

To face the problem that here is raised, let us eliminate at once an easy way out of the difficulty. That easy way out is to regard both pictures—the one we have as a matter of common sense and common experience and the one we are given by atomic physicists—as convenient and useful fictions. The first of these serves all the practical exigencies of our daily lives. The second, applied through technological innovations, gives us extraordinary mastery and control over the physical world in which we live.

Approached this way, there is no conflict between the two views of the world in which we live and of ourselves as living organisms existing in it. We need not ask which is the reality and which is the mere appearance or illusion.

Before the middle of the last century, the theory of the atomists was regarded as positing a useful scientific fiction, and so it posed no challenge to the reality of the commonsense view that a sound philosophy endorsed. Until then, beginning with Democritus in the ancient world and coming down to Newton and Dalton in the modern world, the atom was conceived as the absolutely indivisible unit of matter. In the words of Lucretius, it was a unit of "solid singleness," with no void within it, as there must be a void in any composite and, therefore, divisible body having atoms as its component parts.

We know that in the late nineteenth century, and in our own day, all this has been radically changed. There is no longer any doubt about the real existence of atoms, which are now known to be divisible and to be as much filled microscopically with void or empty space as the solar system is filled macroscopically. In that empty space move the elementary particles that have now been discovered by the most ingenious detecting devices, the real existence of which is supposedly verified by inferences from the observed phenomena, phenomena that cannot be explained except by positing the real existence of these unobservable particles.

Let me make sure that the last point is fully clear. The elementary particles, which are the moving components of the divisible atom, are intrinsically imperceptible to our senses. As a contemporary writer puts it, they are essentially unpicturable— "unpicturable-in-principle." They and the atoms they constitute do not have any of the sensible qualities possessed by the perceptible physical things of common experience. Nor do the elementary particles even have the quantitative properties possessed by atoms and molecules, such as size, weight, shape, or configuration.

Werner Heisenberg's statement of the matter confirms how radical, indeed, is the unpicturability of the elementary particles. He writes as follows:

... *The indivisible elementary particle of modern physics possesses the quality of taking up space in no higher measure than other properties, say color and strength of material.*

[They] are no longer material bodies in the proper sense of the word. *

Heisenberg goes on to say that they are units of matter only in the sense in which mass and energy are interchangeable. This fundamental stuff, according to him, "is capable of existence in different forms," but "always appears in definite quanta."† These quanta of mass/energy cannot even be exclusively described as particles, for they are as much waves or wave packets.

Speaking of atoms and molecules, are we not called upon to say of them what we seem to be called upon to say of ourselves and the other perceptible things of common experience? They, too, are divisible wholes made up of moving and changing components. What about their reality as compared with that of the elementary particles that constitute them? If we could perceive with our naked eyes an atom or a molecule, would we not be compelled to say that it only appeared to be what it was perceived as—a solid, indivisible body—but that in reality what we perceived was only an illusion?

What we are confronted with here is the fallacy of reductionism, a mistake that has become most prevalent in our own day, not only among scientists but also among contemporary philosophers. It consists in regarding the ultimate constituents of the physical world as more real than the composite bodies these elementary components constitute. Reductionism may go even further and declare these ultimate constituents to be the only reality, relegating everything else to the status of mere appearance or illusion.

How is this fallacy of reductionism, this philosophical mistake, to be corrected, as it must be if our commonsense view of things and if a philosophy of nature that accords with it is to be validated?

Before I attempt to suggest a solution, let me make sure that the conflict between the scientific and the commonsense view is clear. The chair on which I am now sitting fills a certain area of

---

* *Philosophic Problems of Nuclear Science* (New York: Pantheon, 1952), pp. 55–56.
  † Ibid., p. 103.

space. To say, on the one hand, that that space envelope is filled with the single, solid body that we experience as the perceived chair contradicts saying, on the other hand, that that space envelope is largely a void filled by moving and interacting imperceptible particles.

The conflict or contradiction here is not simply between filled and empty space. It involves a contradiction between the one and the many. The chair of our common experience, the reality of which a philosophy based on common sense defends, is not only a solid body, but even more fundamentally it is a single being. The chair of physical theory consists of an irreducible multiplicity of discrete units, each having its own individual existence.

If the unitary being which is the solid chair, with all its sensible qualities, is dismissed as an illusion foisted on us by our sense-experience, then no conflict remains. Or if the physicist's atoms, elementary particles, wave packets, or quanta of mass and quanta of energy are merely theoretical entities to which no real existence is attributed (that is, if they are merely mathematical forms which have no physical reality), then their being posited for theoretical purposes as useful fictions does not challenge the view that what really exists out there is the solid chair of our experience.

If, however, real existence *of the same kind* is attributed to the entities described by the commonsense view and by the scientific view, then we cannot avoid a conflict that must be resolved.

A clue or hint that leads to the solution is contained in the italicized words in the preceding statement: "of the same kind." Both the solid chair and the imperceptible particles have real existence, but their reality is not of the same kind, not of the same order or degree. By virtue of that fact, the conflict can be resolved. The contradiction is then seen to be only apparent.

The problem would be insoluble if the two assertions to be reconciled stood in relation to one another in the same way that the statement that Jones is sitting in a particular chair at a particular time stands to the statement that Smith is sitting in

the same chair at the same time, and is not sitting on top of
Jones or on the arm of the chair, but exactly where Jones is
sitting. The statements about Jones and Smith cannot both be
true. They cannot be reconciled.

The assertion about the nuclear particles as the imperceptible constituents of the chair and the assertion about the perceptible solid chair as an individual thing, both occupying the
same space, can be reconciled on condition that we recognize
different grades or degrees of reality.

Werner Heisenberg used the term *potentia*—potentialities
for being—to describe the very low, perhaps even the least,
degree of reality that can be possessed by elementary particles.
He wrote:

*. . . In the experiments about atomic events we have to do with
things and facts, with phenomena that are just as real as any
phenomena in daily life. But the atoms or the elementary particles themselves are* not as real; *they form a world of potentialities or possibilities rather than one of things or facts.*††

Heisenberg, in saying that the elementary particles are *not as
real* as the perceptible individual things of daily life, does not
deny that they still have some reality.

The merely possible, that which has no actual existence at
all, has no reality. That which has some potentiality for existence and tends toward existence has some, perhaps the least,
degree of reality. It is barely more than merely possible.

Let me now summarize the solution of the problem, which
corrects the philosophical mistake that arises from the fallacy of
reductionism. It involves two steps.

(1) The reality of the elementary particles of nuclear physics
cannot be reconciled with the reality of the chair as an individual sensible substance if both the particles and the chair are
asserted to have the same mode of existence or grade of being.
The same thing can also be said about the nuclear particles and
the atoms of which they are component parts. The particles are
less real than the atoms; that is, they have less actuality. This,

††*Physics and Philosophy* (New York: Harper & Brothers, 1958), p. 186.

I take it, is the meaning of Heisenberg's statement that the particles are in a state of *potentia*—"possibilities for being or tendencies for being."

(2) The mode of being of the material constituents of a physical body cannot be the same when those constituents exist in isolation and when they enter into the constitution of an actual body. Thus, when the chair exists actually as one body, the multitude of atoms and elementary particles which constitute it exist only virtually. Since their existence is only virtual, so is their multiplicity; and their virtual multiplicity is not incompatible with the actual unity of the chair. Again, the same thing can also be said about a single atom and the nuclear particles which constitute it; or about a single molecule and the various atoms which constitute it. When an atom or a molecule actually exists as a unit of matter, its material constituents have only virtual existence and, consequently, their multiplicity is also only virtual.

What exists virtually has more reality than the merely potential and less than the fully actual. The virtually existing components of any composite whole become fully actual only when that composite decomposes or breaks up into its constituent parts.

The virtual existence and multiplicity of the material constituents do not abrogate their capacity for actual existence and actual multiplicity. If the unitary chair—or a single atom—were exploded into its ultimate material constituents, the elementary particles would assume the mode of actual existence which isolated particles have in a cyclotron; their virtual multiplicity would be transformed into an actual multitude.

The critical point here is that the mode of existence in which the particles are discrete units and have actual multiplicity cannot be the same as the mode of existence that they have when they are material constituents of the individual chair in actual existence.

If we assign the same mode of existence to the particles in a cyclotron and to the particles that enter into the constitution of an actual chair, the conflict between nuclear physics and the philosophical doctrine that affirms the reality of the material objects of common experience ceases to be merely an apparent conflict. It is a real conflict, and an irresolvable one, because the conflicting theories are irreconcilable. But if they are assigned different modes of existence, the theories that appear to be in conflict can be reconciled.

Not only is the conflict between the view of the physical world advanced by physical science and the view held by common sense reconciled, we also reach the conclusion that the perceptible individual things of common experience have a higher degree of actual reality. This applies also to the sensible qualities—the so-called "secondary qualities"—that we experience these things as having. They are not merely figments of our consciousness with no status at all in the real world that is independent of our senses and our minds.

With this conclusion reached, the challenge to the reality of human existence and to the identifiable identity of the individual person is removed. There can be no question about the moral responsibility that each of us bears for his or her actions.[10]

I think that my solution to the problem is, from the point of view of the philosopher if not the scientist, of indispensable importance. The reason is that unless I am correct in affirming that each human being is, as appears to be the case in our perceptual experience, a single, solid substance, then a whole dimension of philosophy—the dimension in which we find moral and political philosophy—would become null and void.

In that dimension we are dealing with the norms, or the prescriptive truths, about how human beings with freedom of choice sought to conduct their lives and societies. A mere collection or aggregate of particles in motion cannot serve as the agent of human conduct, which aims freely at the good life and the good society.

Human beings with intellects and free wills are the really existing substances that we are dealing with here. What phys-

[10] "Reality and Appearances," in *The Great Ideas Today*, 1990, pp. 318–22. Adapted from *Ten Philosophical Mistakes*, pp. 181–90.

ical science gives us in terms of elementary particles in motion is not the ultimate reality, but only an analytical aspect of that reality. The error is the error of reductionism, substituting an aspect for the reality of which it is an aspect. The whole and ultimate reality here is the individual, substantial human being.

6

Other prefatory matters being covered, I must finally tell readers what to expect and not to expect in the next two chapters. First, what *not* to expect.

A thorough exposition of descriptive philosophical knowledge about reality and prescriptive philosophical knowledge about human conduct and human society would take a library of many books. Obviously, that cannot be done in a few short chapters. I think I have written, in the last fifteen years, some of the books that belong in that library, from which I must borrow some insights, distinctions, and arguments that are indispensable to the purposes I wish to accomplish here.

What are they? Now that readers understand that the subject of Chapter 9 (metaphysical knowledge) is reality rather than being, as it would have been in earlier centuries, they can expect to be given an outline of the contents of reality—what it means to say that something really exists or does not, and what the modes of real existence are; in short, what reality encompasses.

With regard to prescriptive philosophical knowledge, moral and political philosophy, my purpose is similarly restricted. In a relatively short space I can tell readers only what the basic presuppositions and principles of such knowledge are; in short, what errors must be avoided and what truths acknowledged for moral and political philosophy to be soundly developed and expounded.

CHAPTER 9

Metaphysics:
What There Is
in Reality

I

Immanuel Kant, in his *Prolegomena to Any Future Metaphysic*, as well as in his *Critique of Pure Reason*, outlawed the enterprise with which this chapter will be engaged.

He thought he had succeeded in proving that the questions appropriate to metaphysical inquiry were beyond solution by the processes of rational thought, as indeed they were, *if* Kant's understanding of the human cognitive powers was correct, which it was not. Metaphysics does deal with transempirical matters, certainly beyond the scope of inquiries within the realm of experience constituted by Kant's forms of sensitive intuition and his categories of the understanding. Kant invented them to accommodate scientific inquiry, but they were ill-suited for the purpose of metaphysics concerned with a reality independent of our minds, which Kant declared unknowable.

According to Kant, the three great problems of metaphysics were (1) the existence of God, (2) the freedom of the will, and (3) the immortality of the soul. Neither Plato nor Aristotle in antiquity would have thought that this was the case, though Aristotle would have included philosophical theology in his book *Metaphysics*. In the Middle Ages, the great theologians would have followed Aristotle in defining metaphysics as the study of being and the modes of being, which, of course, included the being of God.

In any case, in the *Critique of Pure Reason*, under the heading of "Transcendental Dialectic," Kant sets forth the antinomies in which he shows that the arguments pro and con appear to be valid, and since they are contradictory, they cannot be sound.

Thus we see that Kant is not only the father of all the varieties of idealism in the nineteenth and twentieth centuries, but also the father of nineteenth- and twentieth-century positivism, for whom the term "metaphysics" stood for all unfounded and unfoundable philosophical speculation.

2

Another modern obstacle to sound metaphysical thinking is the dogmatic materialism so prevalent in modern times. Materialism is, of course, of ancient origin—in Greece with the atomism of Leucippus and Democritus, and in Rome with that of Epicurus and Lucretius. The early modern exponents of materialism are Thomas Hobbes and Julien La Mettrie, the latter the mechanistic disciple of Descartes.

The fundamental thesis of materialism is that nothing exists in reality except atoms and the bodies composing them. We can substitute for atoms all the elementary particles that physical science has discovered in this century. Another way of stating the fundamental thesis of materialism is that nothing exists in reality that is not a body, elementary or composite, or waves, or fields of energy.

The crucial word in this statement is "nothing." A quotation from the *Leviathan* of Thomas Hobbes may illustrate this point—the exclusion or denial of anything immaterial or incorporeal. Hobbes proposes the materialistic view that words have meaning only when they refer to physical existences—bodies perceptible to the senses or detectable by sensitive instruments. He writes:

> . . . if a man should talk to me of . . . *immaterial substances,* or of a *free subject* . . . I should not say he were in an error but that his words were without meaning—that is to say, absurd.[1]

The dogmatism involved in this, or any similar statement by a materialist, lies in the negative assertion that the immaterial—the incorporeal, the nonphysical—does not exist. The existence of sensible bodies, our own or any other, does not have to be proved. The affirmation of their existence is inseparable from our perceptual apprehension of them. But the denial that the immaterial exists *cannot* be proved. It is certainly not self-evident. Therefore, when it is asserted, it is sheer dogmatism.

Whether the existence of immaterial entities, such as God, the angels, and the human intellect, *can* be proved is another question. But the inquiry into their existence is certainly not foreclosed by dogmatic materialism.

Scientists in the twentieth century are for the most part materialists. They are not shocked, as I am, by Hawking's statement that what cannot be measured by physicists does not exist in reality. That statement by Hawking is not a scientific mistake. It is, as any other statement of the materialistic doctrine is, a false statement in philosophy.

The words "spirit" and "spiritual" name the opposites of the "material" and "corporeal." But we have no positive understanding of their meaning; we can only understand

---

[1] Thomas Hobbes, *Leviathan,* Part I, Chapter V.

them negatively by using such words as "*im*material" and "*in*corporeal."

3

Affirming the existence of an independent reality, philosophers in the Middle Ages distinguished *entia reale* from *entia rationis*. By the latter they meant those objects of thought that existed only in the mind, not in reality. They might have been called fictions of the mind. They included such things as mermaids, centaurs, and unicorns, as well as all the characters in poetic narratives as contrasted with the persons appearing in historical narrations.

This distinction between *entia rationis* and *entia reale* must not be confused with the distinction between subjective and objective existence. Obviously, Antigone and Hamlet are not subjective; nor are Caesar and Napoleon. The first two are fictions of the mind and the last two are historical persons that during some past time existed in reality, and now exist in the memory.

Anything that can be a common object of conversation between two persons has objective existence, though it may not have existence in reality. What exists subjectively—exists for me alone—are my bodily feelings and my perceptions, memories, imaginations, and conceptions. We can talk to others about them, but they cannot share our experiences of them. These have real existence, even though their existence must always be understood as an aspect or attribute of my own real existence. What exists subjectively cannot exist apart from me. Its existence, however, is real because my own existence is a part of reality.

Careful consideration of these matters requires us to introduce a third mode of existence, that is (1) neither the real existence of entities that have their existence entirely independent of all human minds (2) nor the subjective existence of the contents or aspects of my mind. The latter are entities that have existence in reality because, as my attributes, they exist whether I am thinking about them or not. Their real existence is not independent of the real existence of my mind but is independent of my thinking about them.

What is this third and intermediate mode of existence—intermediate between what is totally independent of my mind and any other mind and that which has real existence because my mind is a part of my own existence in reality? To answer this question I must first explain the difference between instrumental and formal signs. The words of any language are instrumental signs. They exist as visible physical marks on paper or, when spoken, as audible sounds. These physical notations are at first meaningless, and as such, they still exist physically. They acquire meaning, have a plurality of meanings, and can change their meaning from time to time.

In sharp contrast are the cognitive contents of our minds—our percepts, memories, images, and concepts. They are never meaningless; they do not acquire meaning; they do not have a plurality of meanings, and they cannot change their meaning from time to time. Each of the entities named *is* a meaning; and being a meaning, it is self-effacing, presenting to the mind the object it intends or signifies.

If we were directly conscious of our percepts and concepts, instead of being directly conscious of the objects they intend or signify, they would not *be* meanings. They themselves would be objects. For them to *be* meanings and *have* objects, we must be conscious only of the objects that they signify or intend when they function as meanings.

We can now answer the question posed a few paragraphs ago. Though you and I cannot talk about your concept of liberty or mine, since each is private mental content, we can talk to each other about the common object that your concept of liberty and mine signifies. Liberty is a common object of our thought, even though it is signified by two concepts, mine privately in my mind, and yours privately in your mind. You are not conscious of my concept even when you are talking about liberty as an object of thought, any more than I am conscious of my own concept of liberty when I discuss the same object of thought with you. We could not talk about it if it were not a common object of thought.

What kind of existence do such objects of thought have? It cannot be real existence, for it is not totally independent of the mind. Nor can it be the kind of subjective existence that is an aspect of my own existence in reality. Because it exists as a result of being intended or meant by the formal signs that exist as cognitive contents in your mind and mine, let us call it intentional existence.

That which exists intentionally is always something that can be an object of thought for two or more minds. Its existence is not totally independent of minds at work. About objects of thought, except for perceptual objects, we must always ask: Does it exist in reality as well as as an object of thought?

In my book *Some Questions About Language*, I think I fully explained the intermediate character of intentional objects or objects of thought that enables us to talk to one another, both about things that exist in reality and things that may not. Let me quote here the paragraphs that set forth the explanation:

> Were there no middle ground or third alternative, it would be difficult to characterize a mode of existence distinct from real existence and mental existence; but there is an alternative and a middle ground. Stated negatively, it consists (i) in not being dependent on the acts of any particular human mind, and in this respect it differs from mental existence; and (ii) in not being independent of the human mind in general, or of all particular minds, and in this respect it differs from real existence. It is a mode of existence that depends on there being some minds at work, but not on the acts of any particular mind. If there were

no minds at all in the universe, there would still be things having real existence, but there would be no apprehended objects. If this or that particular mind were not in existence and operative, its subjective ideas would not exist, but there would still be objects apprehended by other minds.

Three men are looking at the moon and talking about it. The moon they are looking at is one and the same really existent thing in the physical universe; and the content of their conversation indicates that it is one and the same perceived object that they are talking about. It is an object for each of them because each has a percept of it. Three men; three percepts; three quite distinct mental existences; but the three percepts are the same in intention; that is, while three in number, they are natural signs having the same significance, and hence the same significate— the moon as object. If that were not so, three men looking at the moon could not have one and the same apprehended object as a common object of reference to talk about.

Continuing with this example, let us now suppose that one of the three men walks away. The really existent moon is totally unaffected; but the same is equally true of the apprehended moon that is the object referred to in the continuing conversation of the other two men. Even if a second of the three men should walk away and the conversation ceased, the moon as a perceived object of the one remaining man would still be unaffected; it would still be an object that he could talk about to a fourth man, should that fourth individual come up a moment later and engage in conversation about it. The fact that the apprehended moon is a common object of discourse for any two men at a given time indicates that it can be a common object of discourse again at a later time for another pair of men. If there were no men at all on earth, the moon would still continue to exist in reality, but there would be no apprehended moon. The moon as a perceptual object depends for its special mode of existence on the operation of one or more minds, but on none in particular.

What this example teaches us holds for any other object that can be a common object of apprehension and of verbal reference for two or more minds. It holds for Hamlet and Julius Caesar, for horses and centaurs, for angels and electrons, for events remembered as well as for events perceived, and for objects of imagination and of thought as well as for objects of perception.

Let us consider another example which involves a remembered object that three men are talking about. The three were some time ago among the pallbearers at the funeral of a mutual friend. They are now discussing the fittings of the casket they carried then. They are in agreement that the fittings were bronze. The casket, as a physical thing, was something that all three of them laid hold of; it was one and the same thing for all three of them. The casket, as an object now being remembered, is also common—one and the same object for all three of them. If, during the funeral, one of them had taken his hands off the casket and walked away, that physical thing would have been considerably affected by his physical removal, whereas the remembered casket would not be at all affected if one of the three men who are engaged in conversation about it were to leave the group and the conversation were then continued by the remaining two.

I have characterized the mode of existence that belongs to apprehended objects, which are also objects of discourse, but I have not yet assigned a name to it. In view of the fact that ideas are natural signs which signify, refer to, or intend objects as their natural referents or significates, it would seem appropriate to speak of the mode of existence possessed by objects as *intentional* existence. What was said earlier about subjective ideas (that they *are* meanings; that their very nature *is* to signify) can now be restated by saying that ideas are intentions of the mind. Their intentionality consists in their having significates or objects. Objects, as intended or signified, have intentional existence.

Let me now summarize the threefold distinction in modes of existence which has emerged. I. *Real* existence (i.e., the existence possessed by things) is that mode of being which is totally independent of mind—independent of mind in general and of any particular mind. II. *Mental* existence (i.e., the existence possessed by subjective ideas) is that mode of being which is totally dependent on the acts of a particular mind. III. *Intentional* existence (i.e., the existence possessed by apprehended objects or objects of discourse) is that mode of being which is dependent on mind in general—dependent on the acts of some particular minds, but not dependent on the acts of any one particular mind.[2]

4

In *Some Questions About Language,* I misused the word "idea" as an omnibus term to cover all the cognitive contents of the mind—such items as percepts, memories, images, and concepts. It is in that sense of the word "idea" that, in my earlier book, I was compelled to ask the following very difficult question: How can two or more numerically distinct ideas be the means whereby one and the same object of thought is apprehended?

If, for example, the concept of liberty in my mind, being a formal sign, causes me to apprehend liberty as an object of thought, and that same object is apprehended by you because your concept of liberty causes you to apprehend it, do we not have here two numerically distinct causes of one effect? How is it possible for two numerically distinct causes to have one and the same effect?

I cannot do better in answering this question than the answer I gave when I first confronted the problem. I am therefore going again to resort to quoting my original solution. If the problem itself does not have interest for readers, they may skip the rest of this section and move at once to the section that follows.

> It is important at the beginning to reaffirm the proposition that gives rise to this problem. The theory we have presented holds steadfastly to the proposition that two or more men are

[2] *Some Questions About Language,* pp. 88–90.

able to converse about one and the same object, an object which they apprehend in common and to which their name-words refer. That proposition, in fact, is the theory's point of departure. With that as an unquestioned given, the theory then undertakes to account for the communicative use of language by what it says concerning the role of subjective ideas as the means by which objects are apprehended, and by what it says concerning the role of objects as the significates or referents of name-words, words which acquired their referential significance by being voluntarily imposed upon the objects of perception, memory, imagination, and thought.

The theory, however, also asserts that the ideas that each man has exist only in his own mind. Hence when two men appear to be talking about one and the same object which they both apprehend, each of them must have an idea by which he apprehends that object, an idea which is numerically distinct from the idea in the mind of the other man. If one of the men were to cease to be, the idea which exists only in his own mind would also cease to be; but its ceasing to be would leave totally unaffected the idea existing in the mind of the other man.

This being so, it is certainly reasonable—more than that, obligatory—to ask how two numerically distinct ideas can be the means by which one and the same object is apprehended. Since the ideas are intrinsically inapprehensible, i.e., unexaminable or uninspectable, we cannot answer the question by examining the ideas themselves; nor can we answer it by assuring ourselves in a variety of ways that the two men are in fact talking about one and the same object. When we do examine instances of human discourse in which men appear to be talking about one and the same object, we find that what appears to be the case is not always actually in fact the case. Sometimes, the course of a critically conducted and sustained conversation will reveal that the participants in it are operating with different ideas and so have different objects in mind, objects that overlap in certain respects but are distinct in others. On the other hand, the steps in a conversation which attempt to check the identity of the object being discussed will sometimes confirm beyond reasonable doubt that the two men are in fact using words to refer to one and the same object, an object that is commonly apprehended by both of them.

This leads us to a restatement of the problem to be solved. The task is not to show that two men, having numerically distinct ideas, are necessarily referring to one and the same object when their use of words suggests that they are talking about an object common to them both. Rather, the task is to show how it can ever be possible for a conversation about one and the same object to take place, in view of the fact that the persons engaged in discourse necessarily have numerically distinct ideas by which they apprehend the object they appear to be discussing.

A first approximation to a solution of the problem is as follows. The plurality of ideas, when two or more men are engaged in conversation, is an existential plurality which may be, but is not necessarily, combined with a unity of intention. Your idea and my idea, by which we apprehend a certain object, can be two in number existentially, even though they are identical in intention, each being an idea that functions as a means of apprehending the object in question.

When two men successively utter the same word, the fact that the two utterances are numerically distinct does not prevent the sound they have uttered from being the same word; nor does it prevent that word from having the same referential significance. The case of two numerically distinct ideas would appear to be similar. Though they are numerically distinct, they can be the same idea in intention, just as the twice-uttered word can be the same word and have the same meaning. There is, in short, nothing intrinsically impossible about there being in the minds of each of two men an idea that, functioning as a natural sign, has the same natural significate or referent. Each man has a numerically distinct instance of the same idea, an idea that is the same precisely because what it signifies or intends is the same, namely, the object which it is the means of apprehending. Hence we seem able to reach the conclusion that when the idea in the mind of one person is only numerically distinct from the idea in the mind of another, and identical in all other respects, the two ideas can be the means whereby the two men apprehend one and the same object.

A rough physical analogy may help to illustrate what has just been said. From the negative of a motion-picture film, two prints can be made. If the prints are properly made, they will be numerically distinct but identical in all other respects. If these two prints are then placed in two projectors, the projectors can be so focussed that they throw perfectly overlapping images on the screen; in effect, one image projected from two films. Alternatively, images might be projected from the two films on screens placed side by side, and the most careful observation of them would not be able to discern any difference between them, other than the fact that they are two.

The identity of an object being discussed by two men, each with his own idea as a means of apprehending it, is established by the discovery of no discernible difference between the object that one man is apprehending and the object apprehended by the other. There are two numerically distinct ideas at work here, just as there are two films running in the two projectors; but just as there is only one set of projected images on the screen, or two sets that are different only numerically, so there is only one object to which the two men are referring; or if there are two objects, they are different only numerically and in no other respect.

If someone were to ask why it is that two ideas can have one object, but one idea cannot have two objects, the answer should be like the answer one would give if asked why two children can have one father, but one child cannot have two fathers. In the case of children and fathers, the fact that a father can have many children, but a child cannot have more than one father, is grounded in the very nature of the procreative relation. So, too, in the case of ideas and objects, the fact that one and the same object can be apprehended by many numerically distinct ideas, but one idea cannot be the means of apprehending more than one object, is grounded in the very nature of the cognitive relation which exists between an idea as that by which an object is apprehended and an object as that which is apprehended by an idea.

One point of perplexity remains to challenge the solution thus far offered. . . . I said that ideas, which are themselves products of the mind's activity, produce the objects that we apprehend. Without the act of perceiving, and the percept thus produced, there would be no perceptual object; without the act of understanding, and the concept thus produced, there would be no conceptual object; and so on. Considering the causal relation between an idea and the object it produces, we are compelled to say that, if two numerically distinct ideas can be the means by which two men apprehend one and the same object, it must follow that two numerically distinct causes can be productive of one and the same effect.

It is a generally accepted view that this cannot happen in the physical world. In the realm of real existences, the operation of numerically distinct causes would necessarily result in the production of numerically distinct effects. If two causes were only numerically distinct, and identical in all other respects (e.g., the striking of two matches), the two effects (e.g., two flames) might be only numerically distinct, while identical in all other respects, but they would, nevertheless, be at least numerically distinct. How, then, can we say that two ideas are productive of one and the same effect—one apprehended object?

Two answers suggest themselves, the first less satisfactory than the second. If one were to concede that, in the sphere of cognition, causality operates exactly as it does in the realm of physical things, one would be led to the conclusion that when each of two men has an idea that is only numerically distinct from the idea in the mind of the other, the objects causally produced by those ideas must also be numerically distinct. To this, we must add that if they are distinct only numerically, and different in no other discernible respect, then their numerical twoness can be overlooked, for they have the identity of indiscernibles in all other respects. The two men have one object before them.

It is, however, not necessary to make the concession indicated. Apprehended objects are entities that exist intentionally. They are not physical entities possessing real existence. The difference between real and intentional existence, and with it, perhaps, the difference between the mode of existence that is appropriate to physical things or events and the mode of existence that is appropriate to apprehended objects, may explain why, in the realm of intentionally existing objects, one and the same object may be the single effect produced by the causal operation of numerically distinct ideas, whereas in the realm of really existing things, that can never be the case (i.e., a single effect cannot be produced by the operation of numerically distinct causes).

Fully to understand the force of what has just been said requires an understanding of the role of matter in the determination of the numerical diversity of two physical things that are two only in number or in space-time, and identical in all other respects. If one could fully understand how matter is the principle of individuation, causing two physical things which are otherwise identical to be distinct in number or in space-time, one might then also fully understand why individuation does not take place in the case of objects which do not have physical existence and do not involve matter.

Stated another way, if two objects were identical in all respects except number, there would be nothing to individuate them and make them two in number. Hence two numerically distinct ideas which are identical in intention can be the means of apprehending one and the same object, even though that one object is causally produced by two numerically distinct ideas. The numerical diversity of the ideas results from the numerical diversity of the persons in whose minds they are; but since the object apprehended by the two minds does not exist in the two minds that apprehend it, the twoness of the minds does not result in a numerical diversification of the object apprehended. Nor can any other factor be thought of which might result in such diversification.

This is as far as I can carry the solution of the problem we have been confronting. That solution calls attention to a number of points which deserve consideration; it overcomes certain difficulties while, at the same time, engendering others. It succeeds in solving the problem only to the extent that one is able to understand matters that lie at the very heart of the problem upon which the solution rests, such as, for example, the source or root of numerical diversification.[3]

5

Having established the intentional, but not real existence of all objects of thought, let us now compare the scope of the thinkable with that of the knowable reality that exists independently of our acts of thought. Let us postpone for the moment the further question whether everything that really exists is knowable, adequately or inadequately.

Among the objects of thought that exist in reality, some are mutable and some immutable. The former constitute that realm of reality known as the realm of becoming—of things or entities that come into being and pass away—and that, while in existence, are subject to changes of various sorts while retaining an enduring identity.

As long as they have that identity while undergoing change, they have the inertia of being; that is, whatever are the causes of their coming into being, they remain in being by inertia until counteracting causes terminate their being and they pass away.

All material or physical existences are temporal and mutable beings, but not all temporal and mutable beings are material or physical. Reality also includes contingent and necessary beings; the former capable of coming into being and passing away, the latter incapable of not being; and among contingent beings, some are superficially contingent, suffering transformation into something else when they lose

[3] Ibid., pp. 106–11.

their identity, and some are radically contingent, passing into nothing when they cease to be.

In the realm of becoming, which is the realm of time, the real existence of things is qualified by temporal modalities—past, present, and future. Entities that once existed no longer are actual, but they still have intentional existence insofar as they are objects of memory. But much of the past is not remembered at all, so it has no present reality.

Actual existence is always in the present; and conversely, whatever exists at any present moment in the passage of time exists actually, and may also exist intentionally as a perceptual object or an object of thought. But the content of reality is not exhausted by what once did really exist in the past and what does actually exist in the present, for reality includes the future as well as the past and present.

The future is that aspect of reality in the realm of becoming that includes everything possible. Possible entities or events are that which can be, and may or may not be, among which are those things that, with some degree of probability, will be. The possible is not limited to the probable. It includes everything that can be and may be, only a small portion of which may now have intentional existence—imaginable, conceivable, and predictable. There is much that is possible which we can neither imagine nor conceive; and as *possible* it is an aspect of reality that is not actual. Another word for such realities is "potential."

The fundamental metaphysical distinctions are (1) between that which exists subjectively and privately and that which exists objectively and publicly; (2) between intentional and real existence; (3) between real and potential real existence; (4) between contingent and necessary real existence—that which may or may not be and that which must be. What lies completely outside reality in all its modes of being is the impossible—that which cannot be and is, therefore, absolutely void of being; or, that is, nothing. What once was called the antithesis of being and non-being can also be called the antithesis of reality and nothingness.

When in some theistic religions it is said that God created the world *ex nihilo* (out of nothing) what is referred to is not the nothingness of impossibility, but rather a possible reality that is not actually in existence. When it is said that God could have created other worlds than this, what is being said is that reality includes other possibilities that were not actualized.

The distinction between the mutable and temporal aspects of reality and the immutable and nontemporal involves the distinction between time and eternity. Eternity is not everlasting time—time without beginning or end. The physical cosmos may be everlasting or infinite in time, but it is not eternal. All contingent beings are temporal ones; only that which exists necessarilyand immutably is eternal.

Reality, in short, is that which has existed, does exist, can exist, may exist, and will exist, whether we think about it or not, and no matter how we think about it. To all the clauses in this statement should be added the antithetical modalities of the necessary and the contingent, the mutable and the immutable, the temporal and the nontemporal or eternal. Outside reality is the impossible—the unthinkables.

6

There are still other modalities to consider: whether that which exists exists in itself or in another (i.e., as an individual substance or as an accident or attribute thereof); as a part of an organized whole or as an organized whole; or as the member of the whole that is merely an aggregate, not an organized whole; as members of a class or as a class that has members.

This last distinction calls for one comment. When the mind conceptually apprehends an object of thought concerning which the question is whether that object also has actual existence in reality, the question asked can be answered by saying either (1) that perceptual instances of that class of objects can be found or (2) the class conceptually apprehended as an object of thought cannot be perceptually instantiated, but its existence in reality can only be inferred, or not.

This brings us, finally, to the mention of the great metaphysical arguments: for the reality of God; for the reality of free will; for the immateriality of the human intellect; and for the immortality of the intellectual soul. These arguments, if sound, are, over and above all the distinctions we have so far considered, the fundamental core of metaphysical knowledge.

In each case, the question about existence in reality is being asked about an object that has intentional existence as an object of thought. One could not ask, for example, whether such incorporeal entities as angels have existence in reality, unless it was first possible to hold angels before our minds as objects of thought. That is why the statement by Thomas Hobbes (that the word "angel" is without any meaning at all because it refers to an incorporeal substance) is such a serious error.

If one could not use words to name objects of thought that have only intentional, but no real existence, as well as those that have both intentional and real existence, the great problems of metaphysics would be precluded from being raised. Being able to raise such metaphysical questions leaves open the question whether they can be answered affirmatively. If materialism could ever be proved by well-grounded negative answers to the metaphysical questions that have just been posed, that would turn materialism from dogmatic and unfounded opinion into metaphysical knowledge.

CHAPTER 10

Moral and Political Philosophy: The Good Life and the Good Society

I

As we pass from metaphysical knowledge to moral and political philosophy—from the dimension of descriptive truth in philosophy to that of prescriptive truth—certain differences and similarities should be noted.

The chief difference is that in this dimension, science does not compete with philosophy in dealing with what would appear to be the same subject matter—the structure of reality. It is beyond the reach of science to answer questions about what human beings ought to do in order to pursue happiness and lead morally good lives, and how they should organize their societies and conduct their political and economic institutions.

It may be objected that science does propose some *oughts* to us. In medicine, for example, it tells us what we ought to do if we wish to remain healthy or regain our health; and in engineering it tells us what ought to be done to build safe bridges or highways. But these and all the other oughts that science recommends are merely hypothetical.

They all take the following form: IF you wish to succeed in achieving this goal, or to attain that end, THEN you ought to use the following means to do so. Science cannot categorically propose a goal, or end that ought to be sought, for the sake of which such and such means should be chosen.

It does not assert a single categorical imperative. Without at least one categorical imperative, moral and political philosophy has no foundation.

The similarity between this dimension of philosophy and the preceding one is that, in both cases, philosophy, seeking to establish itself as knowledge rather than mere speculation and unfounded opinion, is afflicted with a series of errors that have occurred in modern times. These must be corrected in order for philosophy to succeed in its effort to provide us with ethical and political knowledge.

In my opinion, Aristotle's *Nicomachean Ethics,* properly construed, is the only sound, pragmatic, and undogmatic work in moral philosophy that has come down to us in the last twenty-five centuries. Its basic truths are as true today as they were in the fourth century B.C. when that book was delivered as a series of lectures in Aristotle's Lyceum.

Of course, it contains some errors. All books do. Of course, not everything it says or every distinction it makes is of equal importance. But when it is carefully read with an eye to its main theses, we are as enlightened by it today as were those who listened to Aristotle's lectures when they were first delivered.[1]

The reason this can be so is that the ethical problems that human beings confront in their lives have not changed one bit

[1] See my book *The Time of Our Lives* (New York: Holt, Rinehart and Winston, 1970), Postscript, pp. 235–65, and reprinted in *Desires, Right & Wrong*, pp. 162–94.

over the centuries. Moral virtue and the blessings of good fortune are today, as they have always been in the past, the keys to living well, unaffected by all the technological changes in the environment, as well as those in our social, political, and economic institutions. The moral problems to be solved by the individual are the same in every century, though they appear to us in different guises.[2]

What I have just said about ethics cannot be said about political philosophy. Although Aristotle's *Politics* is a great book, especially in the controlling insights it draws from his *Ethics,* it does contain serious errors and inadequacies. The errors can be corrected, but it takes the institutional changes that have occurred between the 4th century B.C. and the twentieth century to make up for its inadequacies—things that could not have been foreseen or understood in earlier centuries.

Aristotle's *Politics* must be amended, repaired, and supplemented by later and, particularly, modern writings, such as Locke's *Second Treatise on Civil Government,* Tocqueville's *Democracy in America,* and John Stuart Mill's essays on liberty and representative government. The American state papers, such as the Declaration of Independence, *The Federalist,* and Lincoln's Gettysburg Address, also make their contributions.

The explanation of the progress made in political philosophy, in the correction of errors and in its expansion to include what was beyond the ken of earlier centuries, must wait for later sections of this chapter. Here, instead of trying to expound Aristotle's *Ethics* in summary fashion, I am going to state the indispensable conditions that must be met in the

---

[2] See my essays "A Sound Moral Philosophy," and "Ethics: Fourth Century B.C. and Twentieth Century A.D.," in *Reforming Education: The Opening of the American Mind,* ed. Geraldine Van Doren (New York: Macmillan, 1988, paperback edition, 1990), pp. 254–74.

effort to develop a sound moral philosophy that corrects all the errors made in modern times.

2

First and foremost is the definition of prescriptive truth, which sharply distinguishes it from the definition of descriptive truth. The latter, it has been said earlier, consists in the agreement or conformity of the mind with reality. When we think that that which is, is, and that which is not, is not, we think truly. To be true, what we think must conform to the way things are. In sharp contrast, prescriptive truth consists in the conformity of our appetites with *right desire*. The practical or prescriptive judgments we make are true if they conform to right desire; or, in other words, if they prescribe what we ought to desire.

It is clear that prescriptive truth cannot be the same as descriptive truth; and if the only truth that human beings can know is descriptive truth—the truth of propositions concerning what is and is not—then there can be no truth in ethics. Propositions containing the word "ought" cannot conform to reality. As a result, we have the twentieth-century mistake of dismissing all ethical or value judgments as noncognitive. These must be regarded only as wishes or demands we make on others. They are personal opinions and subjective prejudices, not objective knowledge. In short, the very phrase "noncognitive ethics" declares that ethics is not a body of knowledge.

Second, in order to avoid the naturalistic fallacy, we must formulate at least one self-evident prescriptive truth, so that, with it as a premise, we can reason to the truth of other prescriptives. Hume correctly said that if we had perfect or complete descriptive knowledge of reality, we could not, by reasoning, derive a single valid *ought*. Modern efforts to get around this barrier have not succeeded, first because modern writers have not had a definition of prescriptive truth, and second because they have not discovered a self-evident prescriptive truth.

Immanuel Kant's categorical imperative, which he regarded as self-evident, is as empty as the Golden Rule.[3] I will present the formulation of a self-evident prescription that replaces Kant's categorical imperative, but I cannot do this until I have explained the third condition to be satisfied. Kant's categorical imperative is purely formalistic. The categorical imperative to be stated presently is substantive since it is based on human nature and its right desires.

Third, the distinction between real and apparent goods must be understood, as well as the fact that only real goods are the objects of right desire.

In the realm of appetite or desire, some desires are natural and some are acquired. Those that are natural are the same for all human beings as individual members of the human species. They are as much a part of our natural endowment as our sensitive faculties and our skeletal structure. Other desires we acquire in the course of experience, under the influence of our upbringing or nurturing, or of environmental factors that differ from individual to individual. Individuals differ in their acquired desires, as they do not in their natural desires.

We have two English words for these two kinds of desire, words that help us to understand the significance of their difference: "needs" and "wants." What is really good for us is *not* really good *because* we desire it, but the very opposite. We desire it *because* it is really good. By contrast, that which only appears good to us (and may or may not be really good for us) appears good to us simply because we want it at the moment. Its appearing good is the result of our wanting it,

---

[3] See my book *Desires, Right & Wrong.*

and as our wants change, as they do from day to day, so do the things that appear good to us.

Now, in light of the definition of prescriptive truth as conformity with right desire, we can see that prescriptions are true only when they enjoin us to want what we need, since every need is for something that is really good for us.

If right desire is desiring what we ought to desire, and if we ought to desire only that which is really good for us and nothing else, then we have found the one controlling self-evident principle of all ethical reasoning—the one indispensable categorical imperative. That self-evident principle can be stated as follows: we ought to desire everything that is really good for us.

Readers may ask why this is self-evident; the answer is that something is self-evident if its opposite is unthinkable. It is unthinkable that we ought to desire anything that is really bad for us; and it is equally unthinkable that we ought not to desire everything that is really good for us. The meanings of the crucial words "ought" and "really good" co-implicate each other, as do the words "part" and "whole" when we say that the whole is greater than any of its parts is a self-evident truth.

Given this self-evident prescriptive principle, and given the facts of human nature that tell us what we naturally need, we can reason our way to a whole series of prescriptive truths, all categorical. Kant was wrong in thinking that practical reason itself can formulate a meaningful categorical imperative, without any consideration of the facts of human nature. It is human nature, not human reason, that provides us with the foundations of a sound ethics.

Fourth, in all practical matters or matters of conduct, the end precedes the means in our thinking about them, while in action we move from means to ends. But we cannot think about our ends until, among them, we have discovered our final or ultimate end—the end that leaves nothing else to be rightly desired. The only word that names such a final or ultimate end is "happiness." No one can ever say why he or she wants happiness because happiness is not an end that is also a means to something beyond itself.

This truth cannot be understood without comprehending the distinction between terminal and normative ends. A terminal end, as in travel, is one that a person can reach at some moment and come to rest in. Terminal ends, such as psychological contentment, can be reached and then rested in on some days, but not others. Happiness, not conceived as psychologically experienced contentment, but rather as a whole life well lived, is not a terminal end because it is never attained at any time in the course of one's whole life. If all ends were terminal ends, there could not be any one of them that is the final or ultimate end in the course of living from moment to moment. Only a normative end can be final and ultimate.

Happiness functions as the end that ought to control all the right choices we make in the course of living. Though we never have happiness ethically understood at any moment of our lives, we are always on the way to happiness if we freely make the choices that we ought to make in order to achieve our ultimate normative end of having lived well. But we suffer many accidents in the course of our lives, things beyond our control—outrageous misfortunes or the blessings of good fortunes. Moral virtue alone—or the habits of choosing as we ought—is a necessary, but not sufficient condition of living well. The other necessary, but also not sufficient condition is good fortune.

The *fifth* condition is that there is not a plurality of moral virtues (which are named in so many ethical treatises), but only one integral moral virtue. There may be a plurality of aspects to moral virtue, but moral virtue is like a cube with many faces.

The unity of moral virtue is understood when it is realized that the many faces it has may be analytically but not existentially distinct. In other words, considering the four so-called cardinal virtues—temperance, courage, justice, and prudence—the unity of virtue declares that no one can have any one of these four without also having the other three.

Since justice names an aspect of virtue that is other-regarding, while temperance and courage name aspects of virtue that are self-regarding, and both the self- and other-regarding aspects of virtue involve prudence in the making of moral choices, no one can be selfish in his right desires without also being altruistic, and conversely.

This explains why a morally virtuous person ought to be just even though his or her being just may appear only to serve the good of others. According to the unity of virtue, the individual cannot have the self-regarding aspects of virtue—temperance and courage—without also having the other-regarding aspect of virtue, which is justice.

The *sixth* and final condition is acknowledging the primacy of the good and deriving the right therefrom. Those who assert the primacy of the right make the mistake of thinking that they can know what is right, what is morally obligatory in our treatment of others, without first knowing what is really good for ourselves in the course of trying to live a morally good life. Only when we know what is really good for ourselves can we know what are our duties or moral obligations toward others.

The primacy of the good with respect to the right corrects the mistake of thinking that we are acting morally if we do nothing that injures others. Our first moral obligation is to ourselves—to seek all the things that are really good for us, the things all of us need, and only those apparent goods that are innocuous rather than noxious.

3

Let me begin here by explaining the scope of political philosophy, its dependence on ethics, and its difference from ethics.

The opening paragraph of Aristotle's *Politics* provides a brief summary of these points. He writes:

> Every state is a community of some kind, and every community is established with a view to some good; for mankind always act in order to obtain that which they think good. But, if all communities aim at some good, the state or political community, which is the highest of all, and which embraces all the rest, aims at a good in the greater degree than any other, and at the highest good.

As we have seen in our survey of moral philosophy, the highest good, which is self-sufficing because it is the ultimate or final good that leaves nothing more to be rightly desired, is happiness, ethically understood as a whole life that is well lived in accordance with moral virtue and one that is blessed by good fortune. Hence, if the state serves the greatest good, which is also the complete good, the state is the association that comes into existence for the sake of a good human life. Man is by nature a political animal who can live well only in the state—that is, in a civil and civilized society.

Man, being a social as well as a political animal, lived in families and tribes or villages before states came into existence. The state served better the purposes also served by families or tribes and villages (i.e., the perpetuation of the species and the needs of subsistence). But beyond that, the state or civil society enabled man not just to live, but to live well.

Human nature is the foundation of political and moral philosophy, and the same ultimate good is the controlling end in both. Ethics is thus the architectonic discipline in the practical order, and a sound political philosophy is both founded on ethical truths as well as guided by them.

What in our universities is called political science is a descriptive discipline and value-free, but political philosophy is concerned with prescriptive truths and so is not value-free.

Another way of saying this is that it sets before us the ideals we ought to seek in framing and operating our political and economic institutions. Liberty, equality, and justice (with justice limiting liberty and equality) are the chief values that enter into the political ideal, which calls for the maximization of these values.

The difference between moral and political philosophy is that the latter does not remain the same in all centuries, but changes with alterations in the political and economic institutions that human beings innovatively establish. There is progress in political philosophy, whereas there is little or none in ethics. Errors and inadequacies of political philosophy occurred in antiquity and the Middle Ages. They were corrected by advances made in modern times, advances occasioned by the institutional changes that occurred.

This is not to say that some of the basic prescriptive truths in political philosophy are not to be found in Plato and Aristotle; nor that errors in political philosophy (such as the notion of the social contract and the error of thinking that the good of the state is superior to the human good) have not occurred in modern times. But for the most part, progress in political philosophy lies in correcting ancient errors and remedying the inadequacies that could not have been avoided in earlier centuries.

In fact, it may be said that political philosophy is the only dimension of philosophy in which great progress has been made and is still to be made in the future.

4

In terms of what values can such progress be measured or estimated?

Since human nature is the same at all times and places, even when it is obscured by nurturing under cultural diversities, it can be said that everyone ought to seek what all persons need—the real goods of being treated justly, of having political liberty, as much individual freedom of action as justice allows, and as much equality as justice requires, together with as much inequality as justice also requires. (I will explain this presently.)

In addition, the just treatment that should befall all individuals is not only the equal treatment of equals, and the unequal treatment of unequals in proportion to their inequality, but also the justice of securing for all the goods to which they have a natural right, goods that are beyond their power to obtain for themselves, and so goods that a just government must help them attain. Living under a just government is one of the greatest blessings of good fortune.

For the sake of human happiness, to the pursuit of which all individuals have a moral obligation, the political ideal that ought to be the goal of progress in all civil societies is constitutional government, with universal suffrage and the securing of all natural rights including the right to a decent livelihood.

In terms of this ideal, all human beings will be self-governing citizens, governed with their own consent and, with suffrage, with a voice in their government.

It is extraordinary that so much of the progress toward the realization of this ideal has been as recent as the twentieth century. In all earlier times, inequalities prevailed. Political liberty, when it first came into existence in the Greek republics, was enjoyed by the very few—not by women, not by slaves, and not by artisans, who formed the majority of the population.

In all the centuries from antiquity to the end of the nineteenth century, the oppressed were the majority in all civil societies, and the privileged—those who enjoyed liberty and equality—were the few. Now, in this century for the first time, the industrially and technologically advanced nations have seen these proportions reversed. The majority is privileged, enjoying the liberty and equality all human beings ought to possess. There are still oppressed minorities, but the future holds out the promise that, in the next century or two, the ideal toward which we are moving, with no oppressed minorities remaining, will be realized fully.

I have written a number of books on political philosophy that prescribe such progress.[4] This is not the place to summarize their content. I mention them only to clarify certain terms that I must use in stating the political ideal we ought to realize.

Liberty is part of that ideal, but not liberty without equality: all should have it. Equality as part of that ideal must be understood in a way that makes it prescriptively true that it should prevail. Superficially, equality consists in two things having the same attributes in the same degree. In that sense, it is not prescriptively true that all human beings ought to be treated equally.

But two things are, in a more profound sense, equal when both have the same attributes, and they are unequal when one possesses an attribute of which the other is totally deprived.

Thus, with regard to enfranchised citizenship, two human beings are unequal if one has suffrage and the other is deprived of it. Any society in which the population does not have universal suffrage, with a few justifiable exceptions, such as infancy or hospitalized mental incompetence, is a society divided into *haves* and *have-nots*.

Only if all are *haves* is there political equality. That equality is not egalitarian, since citizens in public office ought to have more political power than citizens who are not office-

[4] See *The Common Sense of Politics* (New York: Holt, Rinehart and Winston, 1971), *We Hold These Truths: Understanding the Ideas and Ideals of the Constitution* (New York: Macmillan, 1987), and *Haves Without Have-Nots*. In the last, the principal essays that I recommend are "The End of the Conflict Between Capitalism and Communism," "A Disputation on the Future of Democracy," and "Lincoln's Declaration."

holders because officeholders have more civic responsibilities to discharge than citizens not in office.

When this is understood, the error of saying that Athens under Pericles was a constitutional democracy must be corrected. In a population of 120,000, only 30,000 had the political liberty of citizenship. The rest—women, slaves, and artisans—were disfranchised *have-nots*.

This clarifies the meaning of the term "democracy" so that it can be truly said that the United States, for example, finally approached becoming a democracy with an amended constitution that gave suffrage to blacks, women, and the poor, who could not afford to pay a poll tax.

These are all steps of progress made in the late nineteenth and twentieth centuries. Still one more step needs to be made. In terms of a decent livelihood, to which everyone has a natural right, we still have a population in which a large minority are *have-nots*. When that natural right is acknowledged and secured, and all are not only citizens with suffrage but also with a decent livelihood, constitutional democracy will be fulfilled by socialism.

Democracy and socialism are the twin, inseparable faces of the same ideal, one in the realm of political institutions, the other in the realm of economic arrangements. Socialist democracy or democratic socialism is a civil society in which all are *haves*, politically and economically, and there are no *have-nots*.

Marx and Lenin held up the classless society as the ideal, but it is not egalitarian, for among the *haves*, some *haves* will have more and some will have less according to their just deserts. This will not be understood by readers who use the words "socialism" and "communism" as if they were interchangeable synonyms. Marx and Engels, who were socialists in the ideal at which they aimed, made the mistake of being communists in their choice of the means for achieving this ideal: they abolished private ownership of all productive property, the means of production. As a result their writings led to a totalitarian government with state capitalism, instead of to a private-property capitalism and a market economy that is the indispensable economic underpinning of political democracy.

A sound political philosophy should be able to demonstrate the prescriptive truth that the ideal we ought to strive for is socialist democracy. The indispensable premise in the demonstration is that all human beings are by nature equal. The only respect in which all are by nature equal is that no human being is more or less human than another. All have the same species-specific attributes or properties.

Human beings are unequal with one another by virtue of the fact that the common specific properties that all have, they may have in different degrees. But this does not make them unequal in the sense that some are *haves* and some *have-nots* with respect to their being human.

In all the prior centuries in which human inequality was falsely stressed the population was divided, not by the degree of the human traits they all possess, but rather by the fact that some were thought to have human powers that others lacked—women, slaves, peons or peasants, factory workers, and so on.

It is only in the twentieth century that fundamental human equality has come to be recognized, and all forms of racism and sexism have been decried. But that has not happened everywhere—only in the more advanced nations. We have plenty of room for further progress in the centuries that lie ahead.

5

How can the extraordinary progress in political philosophy, much of it so very recent, be explained? Human nature, especially natural needs that are at its foundation, has not undergone change. The needs inherent in human nature are the same today as they were in the time of Plato and Aristotle. The answer, or at least a part of it, must lie in the change in human institutions.

There certainly has been progress from antiquity to the present day in our political institutions, and in the economic arrangements that provide their underpinnings. In addition, there have been even more remarkable advances in technology, especially in the last century and in this, changes that have greatly increased our power to produce distributable wealth and to dispense with slave labor—chattel slavery and what Marx called "exploited wage-slavery."

Human love of liberty can be more readily and universally satisfied in the twentieth century than ever before; and it is only in this century that the desire for equality, on the part of women, blacks, and other racial minorities, has lit the fires of revolutionary movements.

Alexis de Tocqueville perceived these changes during his visit to America in 1831–32. His book *Democracy in America* was written at a time when the Constitution of the United States was as far from being democratic as the Constitution of Athens in the fourth century B.C. But what Tocqueville perceived were the springs and tendencies toward liberty and equality that led him to prophesize the realization of the ideal, one that would not only be realized in America, but would eventually sweep over the whole world.

These are the conditions and the factors that may go a long way toward explaining the progress made in political philosophy. Philosophy's recognition of the ideal that ought to be realized in our political and economic affairs is not the motive power of the revolutionary advances that have been made, but it is rather their actual occurrence which made possible a political philosophy that would be sounder than anything formulated by philosophers in the past.

A word more about the part played by technology and the

industrial production of wealth. Consider the statement of natural rights made by John Locke and by the Declaration of Independence. Both preceded the industrial revolution that technological advances fueled. Both preceded the production of enough wealth by free labor and by industrial capital to enable the war on poverty and destitution to begin, to hasten the abolition of slave labor, to emancipate women from the domestic economy in which they served, and to lead to the organization of labor and the power of labor unions as well as to the formation of business corporations.

If chattel slavery and what Marx called the "exploited wage-slavery" of the factory workers was a violation of natural rights, if the inferior status and disfranchisement of the female half of the population was a violation of natural rights, if human beings living in the degrading poverty or destitution of economic deprivation was a violation of natural rights, these truths did not suddenly come into existence in the second half of the nineteenth century and in our own day. Natural, inalienable human rights do not change from century to century, but the recognition of them does.

For example, John Stuart Mill called for the enfranchisement of women in the middle of the nineteenth century, but it took until the first decades of the twentieth century for his recommendation to be heeded. Marx and Engels called for the emancipation of the industrial proletariat from bare subsistence wages in the middle of the nineteenth century, but it took almost a hundred years or more for that revolutionary ideal to be realized fully as far as it is now.

What helped these revolutionary insights to become popularly implemented movements? What sensitized the conscience of the multitudes to acknowledge natural rights that were always in existence but that were not recognized as recently as the end of the eighteenth century anywhere in the world? My answer, which may be inadequate, is technological advance.

Let me use advances in cosmology to explain this answer. The physical laws that govern the movements of the celestial bodies have not changed in the succession of centuries. What has changed are the instruments of observation, the more and more powerful telescopes and other instruments of observation, which enable us to improve our scientific knowledge in cosmology. Without advances in technology, some of them very recent, that improvement could not have occurred.

The natural moral law and, with it, natural rights have not changed. They are as immutable and constant as the laws that govern celestial and cosmological events. But technology operates with respect to natural rights as it does with respect to physical laws, which are natural but not moral laws. It causes a change in us, not in them. It somehow helps to open our eyes to rights that were always there to be recognized, but that we did not see because of the limitations on our eyes, limitations impossible to overcome under the conditions of human life in the preceding ages.

6

Technological advances are also responsible for one more step in the progress of political philosophy, calling for its ideal to be more fully realized. Changes in travel time and communication time have turned the globe into a community as small as a village. All the nations of the world are now so politically and economically interdependent that a United Nations can come into existence and operate effectively in matters that the old League of Nations could not handle.

The next step needed is toward the unification of all the nations on earth in a world cultural community with regard to transcultural truths, retaining the pluralism of cultural diversity in all matters of taste; and along with that advance, the step toward world federal government.

World government is an ideal that was recognized by a

few long before the twentieth century—by Dante in the thirteenth century, by Rousseau, Saint-Pierre, William Penn, and
others in the eighteenth century. In the twentieth century, the
century of two world wars and the threat of a third of even
more global extent, the vision of one world at peace under
world government has begun to appear more and more ful-
fillable.

One of the chief obstacles to the realization of this political ideal has at last been overcome—the heterogeneity that
existed between the democratic capitalist nations and the totalitarian communist dictatorships. Such heterogeneity makes
federation impossible; the units entering into a federal union
must be politically and economically homogeneous. That ho-
mogeneity now exists or is coming into existence in Europe
and the Americas, and it will soon come into existence in the
Far East.

But two serious obstacles still remain: nationalism and,
even worse, tribalism. In many parts of the world, the hatred
of foreigners is more and more virulent. Xenophobia is rampant. It is difficult to say what it will take to cure these
political illnesses, for that is what they are.

The two political imperatives that must win the allegiance
of everyone are the abolition of nationalism and the abolition
of tribalism. But even before that actually occurs, the final
step of progress in political philosophy is to incorporate in it
the thesis that world peace through world federal government is an indispensable part of the ideal that ought to be
sought.[5]

[5] See my essay "The New World of the Twenty-first Century: USDR," in *Haves
Without Have-Nots*.

PART THREE

Philosophical

Analysis:

The Third and

Fourth Dimensions

CHAPTER 11

Regarding Philosophical Analysis

I

We turn now from philosophical knowledge to philosophical analysis—from the first two dimensions of philosophy to the second two.

Readers who remember points made in Chapter 3 will recall the distinction between first- and second-order work in philosophy. First-order work concerns reality; second-order, the intellect's own intelligible objects—objects of thought.

Thus we go from the realm of the sensible that is also intelligible, in which science and philosophy operate side by side, sometimes competitively and sometimes cooperatively, to the realm of the purely intelligible, which is exclusively philosophy's domain.

It is to this realm that, under the influence of positivism, the Anglo-American school of linguistic and analytical philosophers retreated in the twentieth century, where their work could not be challenged by science, as it might be in the realm of first-order work.

At the very beginning of philosophy in the West, in the fifth century B.C., the dialogues of Plato dealt with ideas—with the intelligible objects of thought that Plato mistakenly thought was the realm of being quite separate from the sensible world of becoming, with which the pre-Socratic physicists dealt. The titles of his dialogues name persons, but they could just as readily have named ideas as the subjects being discussed.

Thus, the *Euthyphro* is a discussion of piety, the *Phaedrus* a discussion of love and friendship, the *Symposium* a discussion of love, the *Meno* a discussion of virtue; the *Republic* a discussion of justice; the *Philebus* a discussion of philosophy and truth, and so on.

Only two of Plato's many dialogues—the *Timaeus* and the *Parmenides*—deal with first-order questions about reality and with metaphysical knowledge. By contrast, almost all the treatises of Aristotle, except the *Organon* and the *Rhetoric*, are expositions of what we today would regard as scientific or philosophical knowledge.

It is incorrect to say that ideas are objects of knowledge. We do not *know* the ideas of liberty or of justice or of wealth; we *understand them*. This is the appropriate thing to say for purely intelligible objects.

2

The word "idea" in contemporary English usage has two meanings that must be kept clearly distinct. One is the meaning that comes down to us from Plato. This is the objective meaning of the word, which refers to the objects of thought that have intentional existence and about which, except for perceptual objects, it is necessary to ask whether or not they exist in reality. Here ideas are *that which* we understand.

The other meaning comes down to us from John Locke's *An Essay Concerning Human Understanding* and from all the British psychologists who adopted his usage. This is the subjective use of the word, naming all the cognitive contents of the mind—its perceptions, imaginations, memories, and concepts.

In the case of concepts, abstract ideas are not affirmed by such nominalists as Bishop George Berkeley and David Hume. They denied the existence in the mind of abstract ideas.

Keeping these two utterly distinct meanings of the word "idea" separate is so important that I propose to use a typographical device to keep them distinct for my readers. When I am using the word "idea" in its objective sense, I will use small capital letters, that is, IDEA. When I use it in its subjective sense, I will always put the word "idea" in quotation marks.

3

A word must be said about the relationship between the third and fourth dimensions of philosophy. In the third dimension, we will be dealing with IDEAS directly—mainly the 102 great IDEAS treated in the *Syntopicon*.[1]

Among these 102 IDEAS, about sixteen name subject matters of investigation by scholars. They are:

ART	PHILOSOPHY
EDUCATION	PHYSICS
HISTORY	POETRY
LANGUAGE	RELIGION
LAW	RHETORIC
LOGIC	THEOLOGY
MATHEMATICS	
MECHANICS	
MEDICINE	
METAPHYSICS	

[1] The *Syntopicon* is attached to the set of *Great Books of the Western World* (2nd Edition) published by Encyclopaedia Britannica (1990). With the permission of Encyclopaedia Britannica, Inc., the essays about the 102 IDEAS have been published by Macmillan under the title *The Great Ideas: A Lexicon of Western Thought* (1992).

We will deal with a few of these ideas in Chapter 12, but most of them will be discussed in Chapter 13, which treats the fourth dimension of philosophy, in which we have the philosophy of the various intellectual disciplines and scholarly subject matters, such as the philosophy of history, the philosophy of law, the philosophy of language, the philosophy of science, the philosophy of religion, and so on.

Thus, in the realm of philosophical analysis, the fourth dimension is subordinate to and depends in part on the third, as in the realm of philosophical knowledge, moral and political philosophy is subordinate to and depends on metaphysics, especially in its philosophical psychology, which is knowledge about human nature.

The reason I have used the word "objective" in the subtitle of this book to name the third dimension of philosophy is that the philosophical study of IDEAS is concerned with IDEAS as intelligible *objects* of the mind. And the reason for calling the fourth dimension of philosophy "categorical" is that it treats the various categories of subject matter—the diverse kinds of intellectual disciplines or modes of learning.

CHAPTER 12

The Understanding of Ideas

I

I would like to begin here by listing most of the 102 great IDEAS not in alphabetical order as in the *Syntopicon*, but classified according to the academic subject matters to which they are most relevant. In some cases, the IDEAS may be on two lists. I will omit from this classified listing the majority of the sixteen IDEAS mentioned in the preceding chapter (see p. 147, *supra*), that is, those that name the intellectual disciplines and subject matters of scholarly research.

ANTHROPOLOGY AND PSYCHOLOGY

DESIRE

EMOTION

EXPERIENCE

HABIT

IMMORTALITY

JUDGMENT

KNOWLEDGE

LOVE

MAN

MEMORY AND
   IMAGINATION

MIND

OPINION

PLEASURE AND PAIN

PROPHECY

SENSE

SIGN AND SYMBOL

SOUL

WILL

POLITICS

ARISTOCRACY	LIBERTY
CITIZEN	MONARCHY
CONSTITUTION	OLIGARCHY
CUSTOM AND CONVENTION	PROGRESS
	PUNISHMENT
DEMOCRACY	REVOLUTION
FAMILY	SLAVERY
GOVERNMENT	STATE
JUSTICE	TYRANNY
LABOR	WAR AND PEACE

ETHICS

COURAGE	PRUDENCE
DESIRE	SIN
DUTY	TEMPERANCE
GOOD AND EVIL	VIRTUE AND VICE
HAPPINESS	WEALTH
HONOR	WISDOM
JUSTICE	

METAPHYSICS

ANGEL	NATURE
BEING	NECESSITY AND CONTINGENCY
CAUSE	
CHANCE	ONE AND MANY
CHANGE	OPPOSITION
ETERNITY	PRINCIPLE
FATE	QUALITY
FORM	QUANTITY
GOD	RELATION
INFINITY	SAME AND OTHER
MATTER	SPACE

TIME
UNIVERSAL AND
  PARTICULAR

WORLD

PHYSICS

ASTRONOMY AND
  COSMOLOGY
CAUSE
CHANCE
ELEMENT
INFINITY
MATHEMATICS
MATTER

MECHANICS
NATURE
QUALITY
QUANTITY
RELATION
SPACE
TIME
WORLD

LIBERAL ARTS

DEFINITION
DIALECTIC
HYPOTHESIS
IDEA
INDUCTION

LANGUAGE
LOGIC
MATHEMATICS
REASONING
RHETORIC

TRANSCENDENTAL *IDEAS* APPLICABLE TO EVERYTHING

BEAUTY
BEING
GOOD AND EVIL

SAME AND OTHER
TRUTH

It will be noted that certain IDEAS fall under several different categories, while others belong exclusively to one category or another.

2

I face unusual difficulties in communicating to my readers a sense of what goes on in the philosophical analysis of the great IDEAS, most of which have been listed and classified in the preceding section.

Some of my readers, perhaps many, have never examined the analysis of a great IDEA. Some, again probably many, have never seen the Outline of Topics that, in the *Syntopicon,* immediately follows the essay about that IDEA. They may not, therefore, realize that the Outline of Topics sets forth all the themes or topics about which there has been agreement and disagreement among philosophers, scientists, historians, and poets during the last twenty-five centuries.

Not knowing that, they also may not know that the essay preceding the Outline of Topics presents the major points of view about these controversial topics without taking any position on them pro or con. It is a dialectically detached and neutral or impartial and nonpartisan review of major controversies in the philosophical study of IDEAS.

One more point should be mentioned. I myself have written a number of books dealing with the great IDEAS, in which I have expounded positions and affirmed doctrines; in other words, these were written from a point of view about how issues should be resolved in order to get at the truth, rather than striving to be point-of-viewless in simply stating the issues.

In one book, I have covered Truth, Goodness, Beauty, Liberty, Equality, and Justice.[1] In another, I have treated Labor, Wealth, Virtue, Happiness, State, Government, Constitution, Democracy, and Citizenship.[2] And I have written

[1] See *Six Great Ideas.*
[2] See *A Vision of the Future: Twelve Ideas for a Better Life and a Better Society* (New York: Macmillan, 1984).

books that deal with Mind, Sense and Imagination, Man, and God.[3]

In this book I cannot expound my own philosophical insights and doctrines about the great IDEAS mentioned here, which are the objects of philosophical analysis. That would repeat in summary what I have already written at length elsewhere. Yet readers would be left in the dark about what is meant by the philosophical analysis of IDEAS if they were not at least able to examine the interior structure of the great IDEAS mentioned here.

In order for them to be able to do just that, I have placed in the following section of this chapter the topical outlines of most of the great IDEAS I have mentioned, and the topical outlines of a few others that I thought would be of great interest to readers.[4] These Outlines of Topics do not express my own philosophical doctrines. They are, as said, dialectically neutral or impartial.

A word more must be said about the meaning of "topic." As its etymology indicates, a topic is a place. Topology is a branch of mathematics dealing with the manipulation of places. In its logical meaning, a topic states a theme or issue on which diverse minds meet in discussion and agree or disagree. Everything about which minds can concentrate on and concur or differ is a topic of conversation.

With this said, readers can examine the Outlines of Topics for a dozen or more of the great IDEAS, noting how the topical structure of one IDEA resembles or differs from the topical structure of another and especially focusing on themes or issues that have been the subject of much controversy in the history of Western thought.

Whether the individuals engaging in such controversy are philosophers or scientists, historians, mathematicians, or po-

---

[3] See *Intellect: Mind Over Matter,* and *How to Think About God: A Guide for the 20th Century Pagan* (New York: Macmillan, 1980, paperback edition, 1991).
[4] For convenience, I have placed the Outlines of Topics in alphabetical order.

ets, the controversies themselves are all philosophical. Those
engaging in them who do not think of themselves as philosophers are, nevertheless, thinking philosophically about the
great IDEAS.

The analysis of IDEAS is a dimension of philosophy, not
the business of science, history, mathematics, or poetry.
Those engaged in other intellectual disciplines have to become philosophical when they engage with philosophers in
the study of the great IDEAS, which is the proper business of
philosophers when they work in its third dimension.

3

Before I ask readers to examine a selected set of Outlines of
Topics, each of which constitutes the inner structure of a
great IDEA, set forth in Section 4, I should explain why I am
presenting these outlines to readers for their examination.

In the first place, these outlines are *not* the substance of
philosophy's third dimension. They are not doctrinal, but
rather dialectical. The philosophical doctrines that result
from the study of the great IDEAS are to be found in books
that deal with them and state a sound and satisfactory understanding of one or more of the great IDEAS. In the course
of my career as a philosopher, I have written such books.

In the second place, without examining the Outlines of
Topics that are presented in Section 4, readers are not likely
to understand the point made earlier: that when they use the
word "idea" in its subjective sense, they are always referring
to concepts in their own minds, concepts that are always the
id quo (*that by which* we think intellectually), never the *id
quod*, the intelligible objects of thought (*that which* we study
philosophically in philosophy's third dimension). I have sug-
gested that whenever the word "idea" appears in quotation
marks it is being used to signify the word's subjective sense;
and whenever the word appears in small capital letters I am

referring to objects of thought which, in philosophy's third dimension, are to be studied. More or less correct, more or less sound and adequate, theories that state an understanding of such intelligible objects may result from such study.

In the third place, the great IDEAS are the common objects commented on and discussed by the authors of the great books—those authors who are the leading representatives of the intellectual and cultural tradition of Western civilization. The function the *Syntopicon* discharged was to provide orderly access to what these authors have to say about this or that topic to be found in the structure of the great IDEAS.

Hence, in the fourth place, if different authors had been considered, it might have been necessary to add other topics or to reformulate certain topics. But, from the point of view of philosophy's third dimension, such changes would be of minor consequence.

In the fifth place, readers should remember that the Outlines of Topics are dialectically constructed; in other words, they represent a thoroughly nonpartisan or impartial statement of the issues that have arisen with respect to each of the great IDEAS. Each topic is so worded that it states, point of viewlessly, all differing points of view about the matter under consideration. Each topic is the place where the great conversation occurs—where the authors can be cited differing, disagreeing, and arguing pro and con.

In the sixth place, Outlines of Topics are, in a sense, maps of the controversies that have occurred in philosophy's third dimension. The dialectical account of such controversies, such as the one provided in my two volumes on the IDEA of freedom,[5] represents a cooperative venture, clarifying what has been thought about the subject and serving as a preparation that any philosopher needs when he or she writes a book that is a doctrinal account of the IDEA of freedom, or of

[5] *The Idea of Freedom.*

freedom as an object of thought. Not enough such dialectical work has been done, though doing it is indispensable to progress in philosophy's third dimension.

If readers will bear all these points in mind, I think they will find it useful to examine carefully the selected Outlines of Topics presented in the following section.[6]

---

[6] Outlines of Topics taken from *The Syntopicon: An Index to the Great Ideas,* in *Great Books of the Western World* (2nd Edition). Reprinted by permission from *Great Books of the Western World,* © 1990 by Encyclopaedia Britannica, Inc.

4

GOD

1. The polytheistic conception of the supernatural order
   1a. The nature and existence of the gods
   1b. The hierarchy of the gods: their relation to one another
   1c. The intervention of the gods in the affairs of men: their judgment of the deserts of men
2. The existence of one God
   2a. The revelation of one God
   2b. The evidences and proofs of God's existence
   2c. Criticisms of the proofs of God's existence: agnosticism
   2d. The postulation of God: practical grounds for belief
3. Man's relation to God or the gods
   3a. The fear of God or the gods
   3b. The reproach or defiance of God or the gods
   3c. The love of God or the gods
   3d. Obedience to God or the gods: the trials of individuals by God
   3e. The worship of God or the gods: prayer, propitiation, sacrifice
   3f. The imitation of God or the gods: the divine element in human nature; the deification of men; man as the image of God
4. The divine nature in itself: the divine attributes
   4a. The identity of essence and existence in God: the necessity of a being whose essence involves its existence
   4b. The unity and simplicity of the divine nature

7. Doctrines common to the Jewish, Islamic, and Christian conceptions of God and His relation to the world and man
   - 7a. Creation
   - 7b. Providence
   - 7c. Divine government and law
   - 7d. Grace
   - 7e. Miracles
   - 7f. The Book of Life
   - 7g. The resurrection of the body
   - 7h. The Last Judgment and the end of the world

8. Specifically Jewish doctrines concerning God and His people
   - 8a. The Chosen People: Jew and gentile
   - 8b. God's Covenant with Israel: circumcision as sign of the Covenant
   - 8c. The Law: its observance as a condition of righteousness and blessedness
   - 8d. The Temple: the Ark of the Torah
   - 8e. The messianic hope

9. Specifically Christian dogmas concerning the divine nature and human destiny
   - 9a. The persons of the Trinity: Father, Son, Holy Spirit
   - 9b. The Incarnation: the God-man
     - (1) The divinity of Christ
     - (2) The humanity of Christ
     - (3) Mary, the Mother of God
   - 9c. Christ the Saviour and Redeemer: the resurrection and ascension of Christ; the doctrines of original sin and salvation
   - 9d. The Church: the mystical body of Christ; the Apostolate
   - 9e. The sacraments

GOOD AND EVIL

OUTLINE OF TOPICS

1. The general theory of good and evil
   1a. The idea of the good: the notion of finality
   1b. Goodness in proportion to being: the grades of perfection and the goodness of order
   1c. The good, the true, and the beautiful
   1d. The origin, nature, and existence of evil
2. The goodness or perfection of God: the plenitude of the divine being
   2a. God's goodness as diffusive, causing the goodness of things: God's love
   2b. The divine goodness and the problem of evil
3. The moral theory of the good: the distinction between the moral and the metaphysical good
   3a. Human nature and the determination of the good for man: the real and the apparent good; particular goods and the good in general
   3b. Goodness in the order of freedom and will
      (1) The prescriptions of duty
      (2) The good will: its conditions and consequences
   3c. The good and desire: goodness causing movements of desire and desire causing estimations of goodness
   3d. Pleasure as *the* good, *a* good, or *feeling* good
   3e. Right and wrong: the social incidence of the good; doing or suffering good and evil
   3f. The sources of evil in human life
4. Divisions of the human good
   4a. Sensible and intelligible goods
   4b. Useful and enjoyable goods: good for an end and good in itself

HAPPINESS

Outline of Topics

1. The desire for happiness: its naturalness and universality
2. The understanding of happiness: definitions and myths
    2a. The marks of a happy man, the quality of a happy life
    2b. The content of a happy life: the parts or constituents of happiness
        (1) The contribution of the goods of fortune to happiness: wealth, health, longevity
        (2) Pleasure and happiness
        (3) Virtue in relation to happiness
        (4) The role of honor in happiness
        (5) The importance of friendship and love for happiness
        (6) The effect of political power or status on happiness
        (7) The function of knowledge and wisdom in the happy life: the place of speculative activity and contemplation
3. The argument concerning happiness as a first principle of morality: the conflicting claims of duty and happiness
4. The pursuit of happiness
    4a. Man's capacity for happiness: differences in human nature with respect to happiness
    4b. The attainability of happiness: the fear of death and the tragic view of human life

5. The social aspects of happiness: the doctrine of the common good
   5a. The happiness of the individual in relation to the happiness or good of other men
   5b. The happiness of the individual in relation to the welfare of the state: happiness in relation to government and diverse forms of government
6. The happiness of men in relation to the gods or the afterlife
7. The distinction between temporal and eternal happiness
   7a. The effects of original sin: the indispensability of divine grace for the attainment of natural happiness
   7b. The imperfection of temporal happiness: its failure to satisfy natural desire
   7c. Eternal beatitude: the perfection of human happiness
      (1) The beatific vision
      (2) The joy of the blessed: the communion of saints
      (3) The misery of the damned
   7d. The beatitude of God

INFINITY

OUTLINE OF TOPICS

1. The general theory of infinity
   1a. The definite and indefinite: the measured and the indeterminate
   1b. The infinite in being and quantity: the actual and potential infinite; the formal and material infinite
2. Infinity in the logical order
   2a. The infinity of negative and indefinite terms
   2b. The distinction between negative and infinite judgments
   2c. Infinite regression in analysis and reasoning
3. The infinite in quantity: infinite magnitudes and multitudes
   3a. Number: the infinite of division and addition
   3b. The infinite divisibility of continuous quantities: the infinitesimal; the method of exhaustion and the theory of limits
   3c. The infinity of asymptotes and parallels
   3d. The infinite extent of space or space as finite yet unbounded
   3e. The infinite duration of time and motion
4. The infinity of matter
   4a. The infinite quantity or extent of matter: the problem of an actually infinite body
   4b. The infinite divisibility of matter: the issue concerning atoms or elementary particles
   4c. The infinite potentiality of matter: the conception of prime or formless matter
5. Infinity in the world
   5a. The infinite number of things and the infinite number of kinds
   5b. The number of causes

LOVE

OUTLINE OF TOPICS

1. The nature of love
   1a. Conceptions of love and hate: as passions and as acts of will
   1b. Love and hate in relation to each other and in relation to pleasure and pain
   1c. The distinction between love and desire: the generous and acquisitive aims
   1d. The aims and objects of love
   1e. The intensity and power of love: its increase or decrease; its constructive or destructive force
   1f. The intensity of hate: envy and jealousy
2. The kinds of love
   2a. Erotic love as distinct from lust or sexual desire
      (1) The sexual instinct: its relation to other instincts
      (2) Infantile sexuality: polymorphous perversity
      (3) Object-fixations, identifications, and transferences: sublimation
      (4) The perversion, degradation, or pathology of love: infantile and adult love
   2b. Friendly, tender, or altruistic love: fraternal love
      (1) The relation between love and friendship
      (2) Self-love in relation to the love of others: vanity and self-interest
      (3) The types of friendship: friendships based on utility, pleasure, or virtue
      (4) Patterns of love and friendship in the family
      (5) Friendship as a habitual association
   2c. Romantic, chivalric, and courtly love: the idealization and supremacy of the beloved

    2d. Conjugal love: its sexual, fraternal, and romantic components
3. The morality of love
    3a. Friendship and love in relation to virtue and happiness
    3b. The demands of love and the restraints of virtue: moderation in love; the order of loves
    3c. The conflict of love and duty: the difference between the loyalties of love and obligations of justice
    3d. The heroism of friendship and the sacrifices of love
4. The social or political force of love, sympathy, or friendship
    4a. Love between equals and unequals, like and unlike: the fraternity of citizenship
    4b. The dependence of the state on friendship and patriotism: comparison of love and justice in relation to the common good
    4c. The brotherhood of man and the world community
5. Divine love
    5a. God as the primary object of love
        (1) Man's love of God in this life: respect for the moral law
        (2) Beatitude as the fruition of love
    5b. Charity, or supernatural love, compared with natural love
        (1) The precepts of charity: the law of love
        (2) The theological virtue of charity: its relation to the other virtues
    5c. God's love of Himself and of creatures

MAN

Outline of Topics

1. Definitions of man: conceptions of the properties and qualities of human nature
   1a. The conception of man as essentially distinct, or differing in kind, from brute animals: man's specific rationality and freedom
   1b. The conception of man as distinguished from brutes by such powers or properties as abstraction or relational thought, language and law, art and science
   1c. The conception of man as an animal, differing only in degree of intelligence and of other qualities possessed by other animals
2. Man's knowledge of man
   2a. Immediate self-consciousness: man's intimate or introspective knowledge of himself
   2b. The sciences of human nature: anthropology and psychology; ethnography and ethnology; rational and empirical psychology; experimental and clinical psychology
      (1) The subject matter, scope, and methods of the science of man
      (2) The methods and validity of psychology
      (3) The relation of psychology to physiology: the study of organic factors in human behavior
      (4) The place of psychology in the order of sciences: the study of man as prerequisite for other studies
3. The constitution of man
   3a. Man as a unity or a conjunction of matter and spirit, body and soul, extension and thought

(1) Man as a pure spirit: a soul or mind using a body

(2) Man's spirituality as limited to his immaterial powers or functions, such as reason and will

3b. Comparisons of man with God or the gods, or with angels or spiritual substances

3c. Man as an organization of matter or as a collocation of atoms

4. The analysis of human nature into its faculties, powers, or functions: the id, ego, and superego in the structure of the psyche

   4a. Man's vegetative powers: comparison with similar functions in plants and animals

   4b. Man's sensitive and appetitive powers: comparison with similar functions in other animals

   4c. Man's rational powers: the problem of similar powers in other animals

   4d. The general theory of faculties: the critique of faculty psychology

5. The order and harmony of man's powers and functions: contradictions in human nature; the higher and lower nature of man

   5a. Cooperation or conflict among man's powers

   5b. Abnormalities due to defect or conflict of powers: feeblemindedness, neuroses, insanity, madness

6. The distinctive characteristics of men and women and their differences

   6a. The cause and range of human inequalities: differences in ability, inclination, temperament, habit

   6b. The equality or inequality of men and women

   6c. The ages of man: infancy, youth, maturity, senescence; generational conflict

7. Group variations in human type: racial differences

   7a. Biological aspects of racial type

   7b. The influence of environmental factors on human characteristics: climate and geography as determinants of racial or national differences

   7c. Cultural, ethnic, and national differences among men

8. The origin or genealogy of man

   8a. The race of men as descendants or products of the gods

   8b. God's special creation of man

   8c. Man as a natural variation from other forms of animal life

9. The two conditions of man

   9a. The myth of a golden age: the age of Kronos and the age of Zeus

   9b. The Christian doctrine of Eden and of the history of man in the world

      (1) The condition of man in Eden: the preternatural powers of Adam

      (2) The condition of man in the world: fallen man; corrupted or wounded human nature

      (3) The Christian view of the stages of human life in the world: law and grace

   9c. Secular conceptions of the stages of human life: man in a state of nature and in society; prehistoric and historic man; primitive and civilized man

10. Man's conception of himself and his place in the world

    10a. Man's understanding of his relation to the gods or God

    10b. Man as the measure of all things

    10c. Man as an integral part of the universe: his station in the cosmos

MIND

OUTLINE OF TOPICS

1. Diverse conceptions of the human mind
   1a. Mind as intellect or reason, a part or power of the soul or human nature, distinct from sense and imagination
      (1) The difference between the acts of sensing and understanding, and the objects of sense and reason
      (2) The cooperation of intellect and sense: the dependence of thought upon imagination and the direction of imagination by reason
      (3) The functioning of intellect: the acts of understanding, judgment, and reasoning
      (4) The distinction of the active and the possible intellect in power and function
   1b. Mind as identical with thinking substance
      (1) The relation of the mind as thinking substance to sense and imagination
      (2) Thinking and willing as the acts of the thinking substance
   1c. Mind as a particular mode of that attribute to God which is thought
      (1) The origin of the human mind as a mode of thought
      (2) The properties of the human mind as a mode of thought
   1d. Mind as soul or spirit, having the power to perform all cognitive and voluntary functions
      (1) The origin of the mind's simple ideas: sensation and reflection
      (2) The activity of the understanding in relating ideas: the formation of complex ideas

1 e. Mind as a triad or cognitive faculties: understanding, judgment, reason

    (1) The relation of understanding to sense or intuition: its application in the realm of nature; conformity to law

    (2) The relation of judgment to pleasure and displeasure: its application in the realm of art; aesthetic finality

    (3) The relation of reason to desire or will: its application in the realm of freedom; the *summum bonum*

1 f. Mind as intelligence or self-consciousness, knowing itself as universal: the unity of intellect and will

1 g. Mind as the totality of mental processes and as the principle of meaningful or purposive behavior

    (1) The nature of the stream of thought, consciousness, or experience: the variety of mental operations

    (2) The topography of mind

    (3) The unity of attention and of consciousness: the selectivity of mind

2. The human mind in relation to matter or body

2a. The immateriality of mind: mind as an immaterial principle, a spiritual substance, or as an incorporeal power functioning without a bodily organ

2b. The potentiality of intellect or reason compared with the potentiality of matter or nature

2c. The interaction of mind and body

    (1) The physiological conditions of mental activity

    (2) The influence of mental activity on bodily states

2d. The parallelism of mind and body

2e. The reduction of mind to matter: the atomic explanation of its processes, and of the difference between mind and soul, and between mind and body

3. Mind in animals and in men

    3a. Mind, reason, or understanding as a specific property of human nature: comparison of human reason with animal intelligence and instinct

    3b. Mentality as a common property of men and animals: the differences between human and animal intelligence in degree or quality

    3c. The evolution of mind or intelligence

4. The various states of the human mind

    4a. Individual differences in intelligence: degrees of capacity for understanding

    4b. The mentality of children

    4c. The states of the possible intellect: its potentiality, habits, and actuality

    4d. The condition of the mind prior to experience

      (1) The mind as complete potential: the mind as a *tabula rasa*

      (2) The innate endowment of the mind with ideas: instinctive determinations

      (3) The transcendental or *a priori* forms and categories of the mind

    4e. The condition of the human mind when the soul is separate from the body

    4f. Supernatural states of the human intellect: the state of innocence; beatitude; the human intellect of Christ

5. The weakness and limits of the human mind

    5a. The fallibility of the human mind: the causes of error

    5b. The natural limits of the mind: the unknowable;

objects which transcend its powers; reason's critical determination of its own limits or boundaries

5c. The elevation of the human mind by divine grace: faith and the supernatural gifts

6. The reflexivity of mind: the mind's knowledge of itself and its acts

7. The nature and phases of consciousness: the realm of the unconscious

7a. The nature of self-consciousness

7b. The degrees or states of consciousness: waking, dreaming, sleeping

7c. The conscious, preconscious, and unconscious activities of mind

8. The pathology of mind: the loss or abeyance of reason

8a. The distinction between sanity and madness: the criterion of lucidity or insight

8b. The causes of mental pathology: organic and functional factors

8c. The abnormality peculiar to mind: systematic delusion

9. Mind in the moral and political order

9a. The distinction between the speculative and practical intellect or reason: the spheres of knowledge, belief, and action

9b. The relation of reason to will, desire, and emotion

9c. Reason as regulating human conduct: reason as the principle of virtue or duty

9d. Reason as the principle of free will: rationality as the source of moral and political freedom

9e. Reason as formative of human society: the authority of government and law

9f. The life of reason, or the life of the mind, as

man's highest vocation: reason as the principle
of all human work

10. The existence of mind apart from man

    10a. The indwelling reason in the order of nature

    10b. *Nous* or the intellectual principle: its relation to
the One and to the world-soul

    10c. The realm of the pure intelligences: the angelic
intellect

    10d. The unity and separate existence of the active
or the possible intellect

    10e. Mind as an immediate infinite mode of God

    10f. Absolute mind: the moments of its manifesta-
tions

        (1) The unfolding of mind or spirit in world
history

        (2) The concrete objectification of mind in the
state

    10g. The divine intellect: its relation to the divine
being and the divine will

PROGRESS

Outline of Topics

1. The idea of progress in the philosophy of history
    1a. Providence and necessity in the theory of progress: the dialectical development of Spirit or matter; conflict as a source of progress
    1b. Optimism or meliorism: the doctrine of human perfectibility
    1c. Skeptical or pessimistic denials of progress: the golden age as past; the cyclical motion of history; the degeneration of cultures
2. The idea of progress in the theory of biological evolution
3. Economic progress
    3a. The increase of opulence: the division of labor as a factor in progress
    3b. The improvement of the status and conditions of labor: the goals of revolution and reform
    3c. Man's progressive conquest of the forces of nature through science and invention
4. Progress in politics
    4a. The invention and improvement of political institutions: the maintenance of political order in relation to progress
    4b. The progressive realization of the idea of the state
    4c. The growth of political freedom: the achievement of citizenship and civil rights; progress toward an equality of conditions
5. Forces operating against social progress: emotional oppositions to change or novelty; political conservatism
6. Intellectual or cultural progress: its sources and im-

pediments; the analogy of cultural progress to biological evolution

STATE

OUTLINE OF TOPICS

1. The nature of human society
   1a. Comparison of human and animal gregariousness: human and animal societies
   1b. Comparison of the family and the state in origin, structure, and government: matriarchal or patriarchal societies
   1c. Associations intermediate between the family and the state: the village or tribal community; civil society as the stage between family and state
   1d. Social groups other than the family or the state: religious, charitable, educational, and economic organizations; the corporation
2. The general theory of the state
   2a. Definitions of the state or political community: its form and purpose
      (1) Comparison of the state and the soul: the conception of the state as a living organism; the body politic
      (2) The state as a corporate person
      (3) The progressive realization of the state as the process of history: the state as the divine idea as it exists on earth; the national spirit
   2b. The state as a part or the whole of society
   2c. The source or principle of the state's sovereignty: the sovereignty of the prince; the sovereignty of the people
   2d. The economic aspect of the state: differentiation of the states according to their economic systems
   2e. The political structure of the state: its determination by the form of government
   2f. The primacy of the state or the human person:

the welfare of the state and the happiness of its members

2g. Church and state: the relation of the city of God to the city of man

3. The origin, preservation, and dissolution of the state

3a. The development of the state from other communities

3b. The state as natural or conventional or both

(1) Man as by nature a political animal: the human need for civil society

(2) Natural law and the formation of the state

3c. The condition of man in the state of nature and in the state of civil society: the state of war in relation to the state of nature

3d. The social contract as the origin of civil society or the state: universal consent as the basis of the constitution or government of the state

3e. Love and justice as the bond of men in states: friendship and patriotism

3f. Fear and dependence as the cause of social cohesion: protection and security

3g. The identity and continuity of a state: the dissolution of the body politic or civil society

4. The physical foundations of society: the geographic and biologic conditions of the state

4a. The territorial extent of the state: its importance relative to different forms of government

4b. The influence of climate and geography on political institutions and political economy

4c. The size, diversity, and distribution of populations: the causes and effects of their increase or decrease

5. The social structure or stratification of the state

5a. The political distinction between ruling and subject classes, and between citizens and denizens

5b. The family as a member of the state: its autonomy and its subordination

5c. The classes or subgroups arising from the division of labor or distinctions of birth: the social hierarchy and its causes

5d. The conflict of classes within the state

(1) The opposition of social groups: the treatment of national, racial, and religious minorities

(2) The clash of economic interests and political factions: the class war

5e. The classless society

6. The ideal or best state: the contrast between the ideal state and the best that is historically real or practicable

6a. The political institutions of the ideal state

6b. The social and economic arrangements of the ideal state

7. Factors affecting the quality of states

7a. Wealth and political welfare

7b. The importance of the arts and sciences in political life

7c. The state's concern with religion and morals: the cultivation of the virtues

7d. The educational task of the state: the trained intelligence of the citizens

8. The functions of the statesman, king, or prince

8a. The duties and responsibilities of the statesman, king, or prince: the relation of the statesman or king to the people he represents or rules

8b. The qualities or virtues necessary for the good statesman or king

8c. The education or training of the statesman or prince

8d. Statecraft: the art or science of governing; political prudence
  (1) The employment of the military arts
  (2) The occasions and uses of rhetoric: propaganda
  (3) The role or function of experts in the service of the state
8e. The advantages and disadvantages of participation in political life
9. The relation of states to one another
  9a. Commerce and trade between states: commercial rivalries and trade agreements; free trade and tariffs
  9b. Social and cultural barriers between states: the antagonism of diverse customs and ideas
  9c. Honor and justice among states
  9d. The sovereignty of independent states: the distinction between the sovereignty of the state at home and abroad; internal and external sovereignty
  9e. War and peace between states
    (1) The military problem of the state: preparation for conquest or defense
    (2) Treaties between states: alliances, leagues, confederacies, or hegemonies
  9f. Colonization and imperialism: the economic and political factors in empire
10. Historic formations of the state: the rise and decline of different types of states
  10a. The city-state
  10b. The imperial state
  10c. The feudal state
  10d. The national state
  10e. The federal state: confederacies and federal unions
  10f. The ideal of a world state

TIME

Outline of Topics

1. The nature of time: time as duration or as the measure of motion; time as a continuous quantity; absolute and relative time
2. The distinction between time and eternity: the eternity of endless time distinguished from the eternity of timelessness and immutability
    2a. Aeviternity as intermediate between time and eternity
    2b. Arguments concerning the infinity of time and the eternity of motion or the world
    2c. The creation of time: the priority of eternity to time; the immutability of the world after the end of time
3. The mode of existence of time
    3a. The parts of time: its division into past, present, and future
    3b. The reality of the past and the future in relation to the existence of the present
    3c. The extent of the present moment: instantaneity
4. The measurement of time: sun, stars, and clocks
5. Temporal relationships: time as a means of ordering
    5a. Simultaneity or coexistence: the relativity of simultaneity; the simultaneity of cause and effect, action and passion, knowledge and object known
    5b. Succession or priority and posteriority: the temporal order of cause and effect, potentiality and actuality
    5c. Succession and simultaneity in relation to the association of ideas
    5d. Comparison of temporal with nontemporal si-

TRUTH

Outline of Topics

WEALTH

OUTLINE OF TOPICS

1. The elements of wealth: the distinction between natural and artificial wealth; the distinction between the instruments of production and consumable goods
2. The acquisition and management of wealth in the domestic and tribal community
3. The production of wealth in the political community
   3a. Factors in productivity: natural resources, raw materials, labor, tools and machines, capital investments; productive and nonproductive property
   3b. The use of land: kinds of land or real estate; the general theory of rent
   3c. Food supply: agricultural production
   3d. Industrial production: domestic, guild, and factory systems of manufacturing
4. The exchange of wealth or the circulation of commodities: the processes of commerce or trade
   4a. The forms of value: the distinction between use-value and exchange-value
   4b. Types of exchange: barter economies and money economies; credit and installment buying
   4c. Rent, profit, wages, interest as the elements of price: the distinction between the real and the nominal price and between the natural and the market price of commodities
   4d. The source of value: the labor theory of value
   4e. Causes of the fluctuation of market price: supply and demand
   4f. The consequences of monopoly and competition
   4g. Commerce between states: tariffs and bounties; free trade

5. Money
  5a. The nature of money as a medium or instrument of exchange, and as a measure of equivalents in exchange: the propensities toward saving or consuming
  5b. Monetary standards: the coining and minting of money; good and bad money
  5c. The price of money and the money supply: the exchange rate of money as measured in terms of other commodities; monetary factors influencing economic activity
  5d. The institution and function of banks: monetary loans, credit, and financing of capitalistic enterprise
  5e. The rate of interest on money: factors that determine the rate of interest; the effect of interest rates on the economy; the condemnation of usury
6. Capital
  6a. Comparison of capitalist production with other systems of production: the social utility of capital
  6b. Theories of the nature, origin, and growth of capital stock: thrift, savings, excesses beyond the needs of consumption, expropriation; current expectations of future demand or profits
  6c. Types of capital: fixed and circulating, or constant and variable capital
  6d. Capital profits
    (1) The distinction of profit from rent, interest, and wages
    (2) The source of profit: marginal or surplus value; unearned increment and the exploitation of labor
    (3) Factors determining the variable rate of capital profit

   (4) The justification of profit: the reward of en-
       terprise and indemnification for risk of losses
6e. The recurrence of crises in the capitalist econ-
    omy: depressions, unemployment, the diminish-
    ing rate of profit; business cycles
7. Property
   7a. The right of property: the protection of property
       as the function of government
   7b. Kinds of economic property
       (1) Chattel slaves as property
       (2) Property in land
       (3) Property in capital goods and in monetary
           wealth
   7c. The uses of property: for production, consump-
       tion, or exchange
   7d. The ownership of property: possession or title;
       the legal regulation of property
       (1) Private ownership: partnerships, joint-stock
           companies, corporations; separation of own-
           ership from management
       (2) Government ownership: the nationalization
           of industry; eminent domain
   7e. The inheritance of property: laws regulating in-
       heritance
8. The distribution of wealth: the effects of wealth on
   social status; the problem of poverty
   8a. The sharing of wealth: goods and lands held in
       common; public ownership of the means of pro-
       duction
   8b. The division of common goods into private prop-
       erty: factors influencing the increase and decrease
       of private property
   8c. The causes of poverty: competition, incompe-
       tence, indigence, expropriation, unemployment;

the poverty of the proletariat as dispossessed of the instruments of production

8d. Laws concerning poverty: the poor laws, the dole

9. Political economy: the nature of the science of economics

9a. Wealth as an element in the political common good

9b. Factors determining the prosperity or opulence of states: fluctuations in national prosperity and employment

9c. Diverse economic programs for securing the wealth of nations: the physiocratic, the mercantilist, and the laissez-faire systems; regulation of the economy for the general welfare

9d. Governmental regulation of production, trade, or other aspects of economic life

9e. The economic support of government and the services of government

(1) The charges of government: the cost of maintaining its services; elements in the national budget

(2) Methods of defraying the expenses of government: taxation and other forms of levy or impost; confiscations, seizures, and other abuses of taxation

9f. Wealth or property in relation to different forms of government

9g. Wealth and poverty in relation to crime, revolution, and war

9h. The struggle of economic classes for political power

10. The moral aspects of wealth and poverty

10a. The nature of wealth as a good: its place in the order of goods and its relation to happiness

10b. Natural limits to the acquisition of wealth by

individuals: the distinction between necessities and luxuries

10c. Temperance and intemperance with respect to wealth: liberality, magnificence, miserliness, avarice; the corrupting influence of excessive wealth

10d. The principles of justice with respect to wealth and property: fair wages and prices

10e. The precepts of charity with respect to wealth

(1) Almsgiving to the needy and the impoverished

(2) The religious vow of poverty: voluntary poverty

(3) The choice between God and Mammon: the love of money as the root of all evil; the secularizing impact of affluence

11. Economic determinism: the economic interpretation of history

12. Economic progress: advances with respect to both efficiency and justice

5

You have now examined twelve of the 102 Outlines of Topics. All of the others differ, one from another, as much as these twelve differ from one another.

Each IDEA has its own structure, containing some topics under which readers can expect to find some philosophers agreeing and some differing, and other topics under which readers will find philosophers disputing about issues raised.

The Institute for Philosophical Research has worked to produce dialectical treatments of five IDEAS: FREEDOM (or LIBERTY), HAPPINESS, LOVE, JUSTICE, and PROGRESS. It would take a very long time, indeed, to produce similarly dialectical treatments of the rest of the 102 IDEAS.

As I have pointed out earlier, I have written a number of books about some of these IDEAS. Other books, differing from mine in the positions they take, have been written about the same IDEAS. If such books were to be written about all the great IDEAS, that would be quite a library, one that does not now exist, except for the few books that make a start in that direction.

I am not referring to works on the history of IDEAS. I am thinking of works that try to advance the pursuit of truth in this third dimension of philosophy.

Some work in this third dimension of philosophy was done in Greek antiquity, mainly by Plato. None was done in the Middle Ages, and very little in modern times. It is in this third dimension that philosophy has a rich future to which to look forward.

CHAPTER 13

The Understanding

of Subjects

I

Among the 102 great IDEAS are IDEAS about various subject matters and intellectual disciplines. A list of these follows:

ART	MATHEMATICS
EDUCATION	MEDICINE
HISTORY	PHILOSOPHY
LANGUAGE	POETRY
LAW	RELIGION
LOGIC	SCIENCE

The third dimension of philosophy lays the foundation for the fourth. It is the understanding of the aforementioned IDEAS that guides the production of treatises entitled "The Philosophy of. . . ." A great encyclopedia will have articles on the philosophy of all or most of the subjects listed here, and to those articles will be attached bibliographies of books that are "philosophies of. . . ."

That being the case, in the following section I will place, in alphabetical order, the Outlines of Topics dealing with

IDEAS of the diverse categories of subject matter—the intellectual disciplines about which many philosophical books have been written.[1]

[1] Outlines of Topics taken from *The Syntopicon: An Index to the Great Ideas*, in *Great Books of the Western World* (2nd Edition). Reprinted by permission from *Great Books of the Western World*. © 1990 by Encyclopaedia Britannica, Inc.

ART

OUTLINE OF TOPICS

1. The generic notion of art: skill of mind in making
2. Art and nature
   2a. Causation in art and nature: artistic production compared with natural generation
   2b. The role of matter and form in artistic and natural production: beauty versus utility
   2c. The natural and the artificial as respectively the work of God and man
3. Art as imitation
4. Diverse classifications of the arts: useful and fine, liberal and servile
5. The sources of art in experience, imagination, and inspiration
6. Art and science
   6a. The comparison and distinction of art and science
   6b. The liberal arts as productive of science: means and methods of achieving knowledge
   6c. Art as the application of science: the productive powers of knowledge
7. The enjoyment of the fine arts
   7a. Art as a source of pleasure or delight
   7b. The judgment of excellence in art
8. Art and emotion: expression, purgation, sublimation
9. The useful arts
   9a. The use of nature by art: agriculture, medicine, teaching
   9b. The production of wealth: the industrial arts
   9c. The arts of war
   9d. The arts of government
10. The moral and political significance of the arts

10a. The influence of the arts on character and citizenship: the role of the arts in the training of youth

10b. The regulation of the arts by the state or by religion: the problem of censorship

11. Myths and theories concerning the origin of the arts

12. The history of the arts: progress in art as measuring stages of civilization

EDUCATION

7. Religious education
   7a. God as teacher: divine revelation and inspiration
   7b. The teaching function of the church, of priests and prophets
8. Education and the state
   8a. The educational responsibility of the family and the state
   8b. The economic support of educational institutions
   8c. The political regulation and censorship of education
   8d. The training of the prince, the statesman, the citizen, the proletariat: aristocratic and democratic theories of education
9. Historical and biographical observations concerning the institutions and practices of education

HISTORY

OUTLINE OF TOPICS

1. History as knowledge and as literature: its kinds and divisions; its distinction from poetry, myth, philosophy, and science
2. The light and lesson of history: its role in the education of the mind and in the guidance of human conduct
3. The writing of history: research and narration; the influence of poetry
    3a. The determination and choice of fact: the classification of historical data
    3b. The explanation or interpretation of historic fact: the historian's treatment of causes
4. The philosophy of history
    4a. Theories of causation in the historical process
        (1) The alternatives of fate or freedom, necessity or chance
        (2) Material forces in history: economic, physical, and geographic factors
        (3) World history as the development of Spirit: the stages of the dialectic of history
        (4) The role of the individual in history: the great man, hero, or leader
    4b. The laws and patterns of historical change: cycles, progress, evolution
    4c. The spirit of the time as conditioning the politics and culture of a period
5. The theology of history
    5a. The relation of the gods or God to human history: the dispensations of providence
    5b. The city of God and the city of man; church and state

LANGUAGE

Outline of Topics

1. The nature and functions of language: the speech of men and brutes
    1a. The role of language in thought and behavior
    1b. The service of language to society: linguistic forms and social structure
2. Theories of the origin of language
    2a. The hypothesis of one natural language for all men
    2b. The genesis of conventional languages: the origin of alphabets
3. The growth of language
    3a. The acquisition of language: the invention of words and the proliferation of meanings
    3b. The spoken and written word in the development of language
    3c. Tradition and the life of languages: language games
4. The art of grammar
    4a. Syntax: the parts and units of speech
    4b. Standards of correctness in the use of language: grammatical errors
5. The imperfections of language: failures in communication
    5a. The abuse of words: ambiguity, imprecision, obscurity; the corruption of language for political motives
    5b. Insignificant speech: meaninglessness, absurdity
    5c. The difficulties of using language in the describing of reality
6. The improvement of speech: the ideal of a perfect language

7. Grammar and logic: the formulation and statement of knowledge
8. Grammar and rhetoric: the effective use of language in teaching and persuasion
9. The language of poetry: the poet's enchantment with language
10. The language of things and events: the book of nature; the symbolism of dreams; prophetic signs
11. Immediate communication: the speech of angels and the gift of tongues
12. The language of God or the gods: the deliverances of the oracles; the inspiration, revelation and interpretation of Sacred Scripture

LAW

Outline of Topics

1. The definition of law
   1a. The end of law: peace, order, and the common good
   1b. Law in relation to reason or will
   1c. The authority and power needed for making law
   1d. The promulgation of law: the need and the manner of its declaration
2. The major kinds of law: comparison of human, natural, and divine law; comparison of natural and positive, innate and acquired, private and public, abstract and civil rights
3. The divine law
   3a. The eternal law in the divine government of the universe: the law in the nature of all creatures
      (1) The natural moral law as the eternal law in human nature
      (2) The distinction between the eternal law and the positive commandments of God
   3b. The divine positive law: the difference between the law revealed in the Old and the New Testaments
      (1) Law in the Old Testament: the moral, the judicial, and the ceremonial precepts of the Old Law
      (2) Law in the New Testament: the law of love and grace; ceremonial precepts of the New Law
4. The natural law
   4a. The law of reason or the moral law: the order and habits of its principles

4b. The law of men living in a state of nature

4c. The *a priori* principles of innate or abstract right: universal law in the order of freedom; the objectification of the will

4d. The natural law as underlying the precepts of virtue: its relation to the moral precepts of divine law

4e. The relation of natural law to natural rights and natural justice

4f. The relation of natural law to civil or municipal law: the state of nature and the regulations of the civil state

4g. The relation of natural law to the law of nations and to international law: sovereign states and the state of nature

4h. The precepts of the natural law and the condition of the state of nature with respect to slavery and property

5. The human or positive law: the sanction of coercive force

5a. The difference between laws and decrees

5b. The kinds or divisions of positive law

5c. The justice of positive law: the standards of natural law and constitutionality

5d. The origins of positive law in the legislative process: the function of the legislator

5e. The mutability or variability of positive law: the maintenance or change of laws

5f. The relation of positive law to custom

5g. The application of positive law to cases: the casuistry of the judicial process; the conduct of a trial; the administration of justice

5h. The defect of positive law: its need for correction or dispensation by equity

6. Law and the individual
   6a. Obedience to the authority and force of law: the sanctions of conscience and fear; the objective and subjective sanctions of law; law, duty, and right
   6b. The exemption of the sovereign person from the coercive force of law
   6c. The force of tyrannical, unjust, or bad laws: the right of rebellion or disobedience
   6d. The educative function of law in relation to virtue and vice: the efficacy of law as limited by virtue in the individual citizen
   6e. The breach of law: crime and punishment
      (1) The nature and causes of crime
      (2) The prevention of crime
      (3) The punishment of crime
7. Law and the state
   7a. The distinction between government by men and government by laws: the nature of constitutional or political law
   7b. The supremacy of law as the principle of political freedom
   7c. The priority of natural to civil law: the inviolability or inalienability of natural rights
   7d. Tyranny and treason or sedition as illegal acts: the use of force without authority
   7e. The need for administrative discretion in matters undetermined by law: the royal prerogative
   7f. The juridical conception of the person: the legal personality of the state and other corporations
8. Historical observations on the development of law and on the diversity of legal systems or institutions
9. The legal profession and the study of law: praise and dispraise of lawyers and judges

LOGIC

OUTLINE OF TOPICS

1. Logic as a science: its scope and subject matter compared with philosophy and metaphysics
   1a. The axioms of logic: the laws of thought; the principles of reasoning
   1b. Divisions of logic: deductive and inductive; formal and material; analytic and dialectic; general and transcendental
2. Transcendental logic: the propaedeutic to all *a priori* cognition; the transcendental doctrine of method
3. Mathematical and symbolic logic
4. Logic as an art: its place in education
   4a. The relation of logic and grammar
   4b. The relation of logic and rhetoric
5. Methodology: rules for the conduct of the mind in the processes of thinking, learning, inquiring, knowing
   5a. Mathematical analysis and reasoning: the search for a universal method
   5b. The heuristic principles of research in experimental and empirical science
   5c. The criteria of evidence and inference in historical inquiry
   5d. The diverse methods of speculative philosophy: the role of intuition, analysis, dialectic, genetic or transcendental criticism
   5e. The logic of practical thinking: the methods of ethics, politics, and jurisprudence
   5f. Theological argument: the roles of faith, reason, and authority
6. Logic as an object of satire and criticism: sophistry and logic-chopping

MATHEMATICS

OUTLINE OF TOPICS

1. The art and science of mathematics: its branches or divisions; the origin and development of mathematics

    1a. The distinction of mathematics from physics and metaphysics: its relation to logic

    1b. The service of mathematics to dialectic and philosophy: its place in liberal education

    1c. The certainty and exactitude of mathematical knowledge: truth in mathematics; the *a priori* foundations of arithmetic and geometry

    1d. The ideal of a universal mathesis: the unification of arithmetic and geometry

2. The objects of mathematics: ideas or abstractions; number, figure, extension, relation, order

    2a. The apprehension of mathematical objects: by intuition, imagination, construction; the forms of time and space

    2b. The being of mathematical objects: their real, ideal, or mental existence

    2c. kinds of quantity: magnitude and multitude; continuous and discrete quantities; the problem of the irrational

3. Method in mathematics: the model of mathematical thought

    3a. The conditions and character of demonstration in mathematics: the use of definitions, postulates, axioms, hypotheses, theorems, proofs

    3b. The role of construction: its bearing on proof, mathematical existence, and the scope of mathematical inquiry

    3c. Analysis and synthesis: function and variable

MEDICINE

Outline of Topics

1. The profession of medicine, its aims and obligations: the relation of physician to patient; the place of the physician in society; medical ethics
2. The art of medicine
   2a. The scientific foundations of the art of medicine: the contrast between the empiric and the artist in medicine
   2b. The relation of art to nature in healing: imitation and cooperation
   2c. The comparison of medicine with other arts and professions: the practice of magic; shamanism
3. The practice of medicine
   3a. The application of rules of art to particular cases in medical practice
   3b. General and specialized practice: treating the whole man or the isolated part
   3c. Diagnosis and prognosis: the interpretation of symptoms; case histories
   3d. The factors in prevention and therapy
      (1) Control of regimen: climate, diet, exercise, occupation, daily routine
      (2) Medication: drugs, specifics
      (3) Surgery
4. The concept of health: normal balance or harmony
5. The theory of disease
   5a. The nature of disease
   5b. The classification of diseases
   5c. The disease process: onset, crisis, aftereffects
   5d. The causes of disease: internal and external factors

(1) The humoral hypothesis: temperamental dis-
positions
(2) The psychogenesis of bodily disorders: hy-
pochrondria
5 e. The moral and political analogues of disease
6. Mental disease or disorder: its causes and cure
6a. The distinction between sanity and insanity: the
concept of mental health and the nature of madness
6b. The classification of mental diseases
6c. The process and causes of mental disorder
(1) Somatic origins of mental disease
(2) Functional origins of mental disease
6d. The treatment of functional disorders: psycho-
therapy as a branch of medicine
7. The historical and fictional record on disease and its
treatment: epidemics, plagues, pestilences

PHILOSOPHY

Outline of Topics

1. The definition and scope of philosophy
    1a. The relation of philosophy to theology or religion
    1b. The relation of philosophy to mathematics
    1c. The relation of philosophy to experimental or empirical science
    1d. The relation of philosophy to myth, poetry, and history
2. The divisions of philosophy
    2a. The distinction between theoretical or speculative and practical or moral philosophy: the distinction between natural and civil philosophy
    2b. The branches of speculative philosophy: the divisions of natural philosophy
    2c. The nature and branches of practical or moral philosophy: economics, ethics, politics, jurisprudence; poetics or the theory of art
3. The method of philosophy
    3a. The foundations of philosophy in experience and common sense
    3b. The philosopher's appeal to first principles and to definitions
    3c. The processes of philosophical thought: induction, intuition, definition, demonstration, reasoning, analysis, and synthesis
    3d. The methodological reformation of philosophy: the role of language in philosophy
4. The uses of philosophy
    4a. Diverse conceptions of the aim, function, and value of philosophy

4b. The philosophic mode of life: contemplation and happiness

4c. Philosophy as a moral discipline: the consolation of philosophy

4d. The social role of philosophy: the philosopher and the statesman; the philosopher king

5. The character and training of the philosopher: the difficulty of being a philosopher

6. Praise and dispraise of the philosopher and his work

6a. The philosopher as a man of science or wisdom: the love and search for truth

6b. The philosopher as a man of opinion: sophistry and dogmatism, idle disputation, perpetual controversy

6c. The philosopher as a man of reason: the limits of reason; its supplementation by experience or faith

6d. The philosopher as a man of theory or vision: neglect of the practical; withdrawal from the affairs of men and the marketplace

7. Observations on the history of philosophy: the lives of the philosophers in relation to their thought

POETRY

Outline of Topics

1. The nature of poetry: its distinction from other arts
   1a. The theory of poetry as imitation: the enjoyment of imitation
   1b. The object, medium, and manner of imitation in poetry and other arts
2. The origin and development of poetry: the materials of myth and legend
3. The inspiration or genius of the poet: the role of experience and imagination; the influence of the poetic tradition
4. The major kinds of poetry: their comparative excellence
   4a. Epic and dramatic poetry
   4b. Tragedy and comedy: the theater
5. Poetry in relation to knowledge
   5a. The aim of poetry to instruct as well as to delight: the pretensions or deceptions of the poet as teacher
   5b. Poetry contrasted with history and philosophy: the dispraise and defense of the poet
6. Poetry and emotion
   6a. The expression of emotion in poetry
   6b. The arousal and purgation of the emotions by poetry: the catharsis of pity and fear
7. The elements of poetic narrative
   7a. Plot: its primacy; its construction
   7b. The role of character: its relation to plot
   7c. Thought and diction as elements of poetry
   7d. Spectacle and song in drama

8. The science of poetics: rules of art and principles of criticism
    8a. Critical standards and artistic rules with respect to narrative structure
        (1) The poetic unities: comparison of epic and dramatic unity
        (2) Poetic truth: verisimilitude or plausibility; the possible, the probable, and the necessary
        (3) The significance of recognitions and reversals in the development of plot
    8b. Critical standards and artistic rules with respect to the language of poetry: the distinction between prose and verse; the measure of excellence in style
    8c. The interpretation of poetry and myth
9. The moral and political significance of poetry
    9a. The influence of poetry on mind and character: its role in education
    9b. The issue concerning the censorship of poetry

RELIGION

Outline of Topics

1. Faith as the foundation of religion: other accounts of the origin of religion
    1a. The nature, cause, and conditions of faith: its specific objects
    1b. The sources of religious belief
        (1) Revelation: the word of God and divine authority; the denial of religion in the name of revelation
        (2) Miracles and signs as divine confirmation
        (3) The testimony of prophets: the anointed of God

2. The virtue and practice of religion: piety as justice to God
    2a. Prayer and supplication: their efficacy
    2b. Worship and adoration: the rituals and ceremonials of religion
    2c. The nature, institution, and uses of the sacraments
    2d. Sacrifices and propitiations
    2e. Fasting and almsgiving
    2f. Purificatory rites: the remission of sin by baptism and penance; the concept of regeneration
    2g. Religious hypocrisy: profanations and sacrileges

3. The religious life: religious offices and the religious community
    3a. The Jewish conception of the religious community: the Torah and the Temple
    3b. The Christian conception of the church: the doctrine of the mystical body of Christ

3 c. The social institutions of religion: religious vocations
   (1) The institution of the priesthood and other ecclesiastical offices
   (2) Ecclesiastical government and hierarchy
   (3) The support of ecclesiastical institutions: tithes, contributions, state subsidy

3 d. The monastic life: the disciplines of asceticism

4. Church and state: the relation between religion and secular factors in society
  4 a. Religion in relation to forms of government: the theocratic state
  4 b. The service of religion to the state and the political support of religion by the state

5. The dissemination of religion
  5 a. The function of preaching
  5 b. Religious conversion
  5 c. Religious education

6. Truth and falsity in religion
  6 a. The religious condemnation of idolatry, magic, sorcery, or witchcraft; denunciations of superstition
  6 b. Religious apologetics: the defense of faith
  6 c. The unity and tradition of a religion
   (1) The role of dogma in religion: orthodoxy and heresy; the treatment of heretics
   (2) Sects and schisms arising from divergences of belief and practice
  6 d. The world religions: the relation between people of diverse faiths; the attitude of the faithful toward infidels
  6 e. Religious liberty: freedom of conscience; religious toleration

SCIENCE

OUTLINE OF TOPICS

1. Conceptions of science
   1a. Science as a philosophical discipline: certain or perfect knowledge
      (1) The intellectual virtue of science: its relation to understanding and wisdom
      (2) The division and hierarchy of the philosophical sciences
   1b. Science as the discipline of experimental inquiry and the organization of experimental knowledge: the scientific spirit
      (1) The utility of science: the applications of experimental knowledge in the mastery of nature; machinery and inventions
      (2) The effects of science on human life: the economic and social implications of technology
   1c. The issue concerning science and philosophy: the distinction and relation between experimental and philosophical science, or between empirical and rational science; the limitations of empirical science
2. The relation of science to other kinds of knowledge
   2a. The relation between science and religion: the conception of sacred theology as a science
   2b. The comparison of science with poetry and history
3. The relation of science to action and production
   3a. The distinction between theoretical and practical science: the character of ethics, politics, economics, and jurisprudence as sciences
   3b. The distinction between pure and applied science: the relation of science to the useful arts

4. The nature of scientific knowledge
    4a. The principles of science: facts, definitions, axioms, hypotheses, unifying theories
    4b. The objects of science: the essential and necessary; the sensible and measurable; the abstract and universal
    4c. The role of cause in science: explanation and description as aims of scientific inquiry
    4d. The generality of scientific formulations: universal laws of nature; the principle of relativity
    4e. The certitude and probability or the finality and tentativeness of scientific conclusions: the adequacy of scientific theories
5. Scientific method
    5a. The role of experience: observation and experiment
    5b. Techniques of exploration and discovery: the ascertainment of fact
    5c. The use of mathematics in science: calculation and measurement
    5d. Induction and deduction in the philosophy of nature and natural science
    5e. The use of hypotheses and constructed models: prediction and verification
6. The development of the sciences
    6a. The technical conditions of scientific progress: the invention of scientific instruments or apparatus
    6b. The place of science in society: the social conditions favorable to the advancement of science
7. The evaluation of science
    7a. The praise of science by comparison with opinion, superstition, magic

7b. The satirization of science and scientists: the foibles of science

7c. The use of science for good or evil: the limitations of science

2

As I have said before, many books have been written about these subjects, but I would like to add here that almost all were written in modern times, mainly in the nineteenth and twentieth centuries.

Where the Outlines of Topics touch on controversial issues, the books will present differing and often opposing versions of the subject treated. These oppositions call for resolution in order to get at the truth about the subject being treated.[2]

Taking the third and fourth dimensions together, it is unquestionable that we have here a contribution made by philosophy that is generally recognized and welcomed in the twentieth century.

It is interesting to note that, on all the subjects with which we have been dealing, there is a "history of . . ." as well as a "philosophy of. . . ," but no "science of. . . ." We have many histories of science and philosophies of science, but we have no science of science. None of the various methods of investigation employed by science are applicable to the understanding of the discipline itself.

Books about the philosophy of science, of art, of law, and of mathematics may be written by professional scientists, artists, lawyers, or mathematicians. But when they write about these subjects, they do so by being philosophical about them.

Their special competence as lawyers or mathematicians may be indispensable to their philosophizing about their

<hr/>

[2]This book, for example, might have been entitled *The Philosophy of Philosophy*. Other books about philosophy contradict its main theses. I have written books of essays on the philosophy of education (*Reforming Education: The Opening of the American Mind,* 1988); about the philosophy of law ("A Question About Law," in *Essays in Thomism,* ed. R. E. Brennan (New York: Sheed & Ward, 1941), and about the philosophy of language (*Some Questions About Language*).

own subject matter, but it is not sufficient in itself. They must also realize that they are writing as philosophers, and they must study their own subject matter or discipline with that in mind.

EPILOGUE

Philosophy's Past,

Present, and

Future

I

I have now done what I can to persuade readers that philosophy, by being able to satisfy certain stipulated conditions, can be an intellectual enterprise that deserves the same kind of respect generally accorded science and history, and additional esteem for the pivotal role it can play in education and in the organization of the university, and for the special place it occupies in the hierarchy of elements that constitute culture or civilization.

I think I have accomplished this principally by showing that philosophy can have a distinctive method of its own whereby it can be an empirical mode of inquiry resulting in a distinctive type of knowledge (*doxa*) about that which is and happens in the world or about what men ought to do and seek.

The crux of the argument is, of course, the distinction between common and special experience. If that distinction is valid, as I think it is, philosophy, like science, can have its own limited sphere of inquiry; it can have first-order questions of its own and various ways of testing the theories or conclusions it propounds, including an empirical test of what it claims to know, whereby some of its claims may be falsified. These things being so, I have argued that philosophy can be conducted as a public enterprise, in which philosophers cooperate, adjudicate their disputes, and achieve some measure of agreement.

I have also tried to explain why philosophy is generally thought, especially in learned circles, to be inferior to science with respect to agreement, progress, usefulness, and the understanding it gives us of the world. That judgment, I have conceded, may be quite sound when it is made about philosophy in its present or past state, which falls far short of satisfying the conditions stipulated.

However, the judgment is sometimes made in terms that suggest that philosophy can never achieve the kind or degree of agreement and progress that science so clearly manifests; and that philosophy by its very nature can never be as useful to mankind as science or as valuable a source of understanding.

That deprecatory estimate of philosophy, I have argued, is mistaken and unfounded. The explanation of the mistake, I have tried to point out, lies in the fact that philosophy is here being judged by reference to standards that are appropriate to science alone, instead of standards appropriate to philosophy's own distinctive type of inquiry, method, and results.

Philosophy, as a noninvestigative discipline, cannot be expected to make the same kind or rate of progress, achieve agreement in the same way or to the same extent, or have the same kind of usefulness of which science, an investigative discipline, can rightly boast.

To recognize this is to see that in modern times—with the ever-increasing cultural preeminence of science since the seventeenth century—philosophy has suffered from these mistaken comparisons with science. However, it is not only in modern times that philosophy has suffered from its relation to other disciplines. As I see philosophy's historic development from its beginning to the present day, it has had a checkered career, full of misfortunes and disorders.

In antiquity, it suffered from confusion with science, on the one hand, and with religion, on the other; in the Middle Ages, it suffered from the cultural dominance of religion and theology; in modern times, it has been suffering from the cultural preeminence of science.

Throughout its history philosophy has been led by false aspirations, arising from its misguided emulation of the certitude of dogmatic theology, the demonstrative character of mathematical thought, or the empirical procedures of investigative science. At all times it has suffered disorders within its own household resulting from the failure to understand itself—its separate sphere of inquiry, its four dimensions, its own distinctive method, its characteristic procedure, and, above all, what it can and cannot hope to achieve.

In view of this, the kindest thing that can be said about philosophy in the twentieth century is that its present state reveals it to be, unwittingly, a victim of its past. The most generous comment to add is that there are no intrinsic obstacles to its having a future much brighter than its past.[1]

Such optimism should not be expressed as a prediction, but as a hope that what is possible for philosophy to become, it will become in the future.

2

In the Epilogue to *Ten Philosophical Mistakes,* entitled "Modern Science and Ancient Wisdom," I tried to explain

---

[1] In *Ten Philosophical Mistakes,* I have pointed out the serious errors made in modern philosophy that have resulted in the steady decline of philosophy in the last three centuries, mistakes that must be corrected if philosophy is to recover.

the steady decline of philosophy from the seventeenth century to the low point it has reached at the present day.

In Part Three of *The Conditions of Philosophy* (1965), I told the story at somewhat greater length, but still trying to do so within a very limited space. To do that with requisite brevity, I chose to tell the history of philosophy in procedural rather than in substantive terms. By that I mean telling the history in terms of philosophy's method, its awareness of its character and its relation to other disciplines, especially religion, investigative science, and mathematics rather than in terms of its theories and doctrines.

That procedural history was written more than thirty years ago. On rereading it I find that I cannot improve on it with regard to the main points it makes, though I can modify it somewhat here and there, abbreviate it, and supplement it in this present retelling. Since *The Conditions of Philosophy* has been long out of print and is generally unavailable, I am going to recapitulate what I wrote there, excerpting without quotation marks.

If I thought, *as I do not,* that it is only in modern times that philosophy has fallen into a parlous condition, then I should undertake to depict the high estate achieved by philosophy in ancient and mediaeval times, to explain how and why it is only in modern times that philosophy has fallen from that high estate, and to recommend the ways and means by which philosophy, in the future, can once more regain it by returning to its ancient past.

However, I think that philosophy has at no time ever satisfied all the conditions of respectability and worth as an intellectual enterprise—conditions that I think it *can* and *should* satisfy. Hence, I am going to try to show the various cultural circumstances and other influences that have so far prevented the philosophical enterprise from being conducted as it should be. These circumstances and influences, it will be seen, differ in each of the major epochs of Western civilization. I will also try to show the mistakes that have been made, especially in modern times, by the various efforts to reform philosophy and to restore it to the status it was once thought to have; and the tendencies in the present century which, if developed in a certain way, might substantiate the hope that philosophy can have a future brighter than its past.

Most, if not all, of the misfortunes and disorders that philosophy has suffered come, directly or indirectly, from the state of its relationship to other disciplines, especially its relationship to mathematics; its relationship to religion in general and, in particular, its relationship to the dogmatic theology of a religion that regards itself as revealed; and its relationship to science, especially as that has developed in the modern world.

On the one hand, philosophy has suffered from a lack of distinction between itself and other disciplines; that is, at certain times in the past, the line that should sharply separate philosophy from science or religion has either been nonexistent or shadowy and indistinct.

On the other hand, philosophy has suffered from the tendency to emulate and imitate other disciplines, without regard to the differences between itself and them which make such imitation inappropriate.

I know that it is impossible to encompass the history of philosophy if the story were to be told, as it usually is, in substantive terms—that is, in terms of theories held, doctrines propounded, systems developed, and arguments advanced by individual thinkers for or against particular positions. I propose to do something else, something that can be done with the brevity required.

I propose to deal with the history of philosophy almost exclusively in procedural terms—that is, in terms of philosophy's understanding of itself in different epochs and also its various misunderstandings of its own nature, tasks, methods, and limitations.

I propose to tell the story of philosophy's checkered career in terms of the soundness of its procedures at various times and the adequacy and correctness of philosophy's understanding of itself, without regard to the truth or falsity in substance of its doctrines or theories.

I have not substituted a procedural for a substantive history of philosophy merely for the sake of brevity. Only a procedural history of philosophy is directly relevant to my argument. A procedural history of philosophy will necessarily take the form of applying the conditions stipulated to the historic materials and judging the course of history in the light of them. If it conveys to the reader the general impression that I hope it does, then the historical applications of the argument should also serve to confirm its validity.

3

THE MISFORTUNES OF PHILOSOPHY IN ANTIQUITY

With the speculations of the pre-Socratic philosophers, with the dialogues of Plato, and with the treatises of Aristotle, philosophy got off to a good start in three respects.

(1) The Greek philosophers managed to pose, and to pose quite clearly, many of the fundamental questions of philosophy. The fecundity of the Platonic dialogues lies in this: they raise so many of the basic questions—questions about the nature of things, about being and becoming, about the one and the many, about matter and spirit, about the divine, about knowledge and truth, about language, about the senses and the intellect, about ideas, about virtue and the virtues, about justice and happiness, about the state and the individual.

Neither the refinement of these questions in later periods of thought nor the later addition of questions that open up new lines of philosophical inquiry should be allowed to diminish the magnificence of the Platonic achievement, which richly deserves the tribute paid by Alfred North Whitehead when he said that the whole of European thought can be read as a series of footnotes to the dialogues of Plato.

(2) The Greek philosophers—here Plato to a lesser extent, and to a much greater extent Aristotle—also managed to lay down the lines of correct procedure in many of the respects that are essential to the proper conduct of the philosophical enterprise. The way in which Aristotle carefully considers the questions raised by his predecessors or contemporaries, and takes their opinions into account, is an amazingly clear first approximation to what is meant by the conduct of philosophy as a public, rather than a private enterprise.

Consider these two statements by Aristotle, which eloquently express his sense of philosophy as a cooperative enterprise. The first is from the *Metaphysics*, Book II, Chapter 1:

> The investigation of the truth is in one way hard, in another easy. An indication of this is found in the fact that no one is able to attain the truth adequately, while, on the other hand, we do not collectively fail, but every one says something true about the nature of things, and while individually we contribute little or nothing to the truth, by the union of all a considerable amount is amassed.

The second is from *On the Soul*, Book I, Chapter 2:

> ... it is necessary ... to call into council the views of those of our predecessors ... in order that we may profit by whatever is sound in their suggestions and avoid their errors.

Pondering these statements, it is difficult not to attribute to Aristotle a conception of philosophical knowledge as testable *doxa*. If he had regarded philosophical knowledge as *epistēmē*, he would hardly have recommended, as he does in these statements, a type of procedure that befits sifting opinions and testing them for their relative truth. If philosophical truths consisted of self-evident principles and rigorously demonstrated conclusions, one would not proceed in this way.[2]

In addition, Aristotle is an empirical philosopher in the proper sense of that term; namely, a philosopher who submits theories and conclusions—his own and others—to the empirical test, by appeal to the common experience of humankind.

(3) The Greek philosophers—here both Plato and Aristotle, though in quite different ways—managed to detect and expose a large number of typical fallacies, paradoxes, and puzzles that result from linguistic or logical inadequacies, imprecisions, or confusions in the discourse that is generated by philosophical problems.

What I am saying here is that Plato and Aristotle initiated philosophy, not only on the plane of first-order questions, both speculative and normative, but also on the plane of second-order questions about human thought and speech, especially when these are concerned with difficult first-order questions in philosophy. To the major contributions previously mentioned, they added a third—an amazingly rich beginning of what is now called analytic and linguistic philosophy—a contribution that, by the way, the more learned of contemporary analysts properly acknowledge.

These three contributions can be recognized and given their due praise without any regard to the substantive truth or error in the philosophical positions taken by Plato and

---

[2] For the distinction between knowledge with certitude (*epistēmē*) and well-founded opinions (*doxa*), see Chapter 1, pp. 5–6, *supra*.

Aristotle on particular problems. When we take all three into account, it is hard to see how philosophy could have had a more auspicious beginning. Nevertheless, the circumstances under which philosophy was born and went through its first state of development were not wholly auspicious. I have three misfortunes in mind.

First and most important of all, there was in antiquity no clear line between philosophy, on the one hand, and either science or religion, on the other. The ancients did not clearly and explicitly separate questions that cannot be answered *without* investigation from questions that cannot possibly be answered *by* investigation. As a consequence of this, Aristotle treated, as if they were properly philosophical questions, questions that can be properly answered only by investigative science—questions about the nature and motions of the heavenly bodies; questions about the nature, number, and operation of the human senses; questions about the elementary forms of matter; questions about the species of living things, their order, relation, and origin.

Many of the treatises of Aristotle show him dealing with what we now know to be philosophical questions, on the one hand, and scientific questions, on the other; but he treats them as if they were all philosophical questions. A great many of the errors with which Aristotle is charged were made in his effort to answer scientific questions without being aware that they require a different method from the one he employed in answering questions that are genuinely philosophical.

This is not to say that he failed to resort to investigation in certain fields, especially in biology. We know that he was an investigative scientist as well as a reflective philosopher; but *he* did not know it. He did not separate—and, in his day, probably could not have separated—these two modes of inquiry in which he engaged, as we, looking back at him, can retrospectively separate his efforts at scientific inquiry from his lines of philosophical thought.

This, then, is one of the misfortunes of philosophy in antiquity: by virtue of the inchoate togetherness of science and philosophy, philosophy took upon itself a burden that it could not discharge—the burden of answering questions that did not properly belong in its domain. We can see the particular sciences—such as physics, astronomy, chemistry, physiology, and zoology—in the womb of ancient philosophy.

Philosophy is, historically, their mother; but they have not yet broken away from her and established themselves as branches of a separate autonomous discipline, the discipline of investigative science. Until this happens—and it does not begin to happen until the seventeenth century—they constitute a burden and a distraction to philosophy; worse than that, the errors which philosophers make in unwittingly trying to deal with matters that properly belong to science insidiously affect their treatment of matters that are properly their own concern.

What I have just said about science and philosophy in antiquity can also be said about science and religion; they were also inchoately confused. The ancients did not realize that certain questions were of a sort that exceeded the powers of human inquiry to answer—questions that could not be answered either by investigation or by reflection on the common experience of humankind. Both Plato and Aristotle tried, as philosophers, to handle such questions—Plato in the *Timaeus, Phaedo,* and *Laws;* Aristotle in the eighth book of the *Physics,* the twelfth book of the *Metaphysics,* and the tenth book of the *Ethics.* Certain matters treated therein are matters beyond the reach of testable *doxa.* If men are ever to possess knowledge of such matters, it must come to them by way of divine revelation and supernatural

234 EPILOGUE *Philosophy's Past, Present, and Future*

faith. They cannot acquire it by the exercise of their natural faculties and by recourse to the evidences of experience and the light of unaided reason.[3]

The confusion of philosophy with religion in antiquity has still another unfortunate consequence. Religion, as we have seen, is more than a type of knowledge; it is a group of institutions, a set of ceremonial or ritualistic practices, and a code of observances and performances having a sacerdotal or sacramental character. When these things are taken together, they comprise what we understand by "a way of life." When we speak of religion as a way of life, we think of it as enrolling the individual in a community who share certain beliefs, engage in certain ceremonials or rituals, and practice certain obligatory observances. A religious way of life can, of course, be lived anchoritically as well as communally, but it still involves more than beliefs; it involves observances and actions of a sacerdotal or sacramental character, observances and actions that have as their goal a spiritual transformation of some sort. Whatever the nature of that goal, one thing is clear: the goal of the religious way of life is not simply more knowledge of the type which the religious person already has.

This last point confirms what should be otherwise clear—namely, that such disciplines as scientific investigation and historical research, as we understand them today, are not, strictly speaking, ways of life in the sense in which religion is. Scientists and historians may belong to learned societies; they may have codes of professional behavior; they may engage in certain practices; but all these, taken together, have only one end in view, and that is the advancement of knowledge,

---

[3] The line separating the domain of philosophy from the domain of dogmatic theology and revealed religion was clearly drawn only toward the end of the Christian Middle Ages. Some of the speculations of Plato and Aristotle about theological matters lie athwart the line that separates metaphysical theology (which is a part of philosophy) from dogmatic theology (which belongs to revealed religion).

knowledge of exactly the same type that they already possess to some extent.

What has just been said about science and history must be said with equal force about philosophy when we understand it as a comparable branch of knowledge and mode of inquiry. Whatever the rules for the conduct of philosophy as an intellectual enterprise, and whatever code of professional behavior philosophers should subscribe to, these, as in the case of science and history, have only one aim—the advancement of knowledge, the same type of knowledge that philosophers already possess to some degree. Philosophy is, therefore, no more a way of life than science or history.[4]

Both Plato and Aristotle were bewitched by the conception of philosophy as *epistēmē*—as something much more certain and incorrigible than opinion because it is grounded in incontestable, self-evident axioms or first principles, and proceeds therefrom to demonstrate its conclusions. Both Plato and Aristotle drew a sharp line between knowledge and opinion (*nous* and *epistēmē*, on the one hand, and *doxa*, on the other), and they both placed mathematics and philosophy on the knowledge side of the line. This misfortune, at the very beginning of philosophy's history, plagues it throughout its history, not only in antiquity, but also in the Middle Ages and in modern times.

The subsequent history of philosophical thought was grievously influenced by the exaltation and idealization of knowledge (*nous* and *epistēmē*) over the best that can be achieved in the realm of opinion (*doxa*). Later philosophers,

---

[4] A simple test can be applied. A truly religious person deplores his own moral failings and tries to rectify them in order to bring his character and conduct more into accord with the precepts and practices of his religion. But a scientist, historical scholar, and philosopher may each recognize that he has certain moral deficiencies without any sense of need to overcome them for the sake of serving better the objectives of scientific research, historical scholarship, or philosophical thought. This is one way of seeing that religion is a way of life and that science, history, and philosophy are not.

whether they agreed or disagreed with the substance of Platonic or Aristotelian teaching, adopted the ideal of *nous* and *epistēmē* as one to be aimed at in philosophical work. Some of them went much further and did what Plato and Aristotle refrained from doing; they expounded their own philosophical thought in a form and with a structure that made it look as if it conformed to the ideal.

If subsequent ages had paid more attention to the actual sifting of philosophical opinions that goes on in the dialogues of Plato, and had recognized that the *Posterior Analytics* does not describe the structure or movement of philosophical thought as it occurs in all the major treatises of Aristotle, philosophy might have been saved many centuries of misdirection in the fruitless effort to conform itself to an appropriate model.

The third misfortune that befell philosophy in antiquity is closely connected with the second. It is the baleful influence of mathematics, mainly in the form of geometry.

Geometry provided the ancients with what they took to be the model of a deductive system. When Plato and Aristotle want to exemplify what they mean by *epistēmē*, they usually offer the demonstration of geometrical theorems. Again it must be said in defense of Plato and Aristotle that they never made the mistake of Spinoza and other moderns, who actually try to expound a philosophical theory *in ordine geometrico*. Yet we cannot overlook the frequency with which they point to geometry as an actually developed body of knowledge that approximates their ideal better than any other and which, therefore, serves as a model to be imitated.

The bewitchment of philosophy by mathematics—not only by geometrical demonstration, but also by the analytical character of mathematical thought—is a much more serious illness of philosophy in modern times than it was in antiquity. Nevertheless, the first signs of that illness can be found in antiquity, not only in connection with the illusions about *epistēmē*, but also in the extensive use that Plato makes of geometrical figures and of numbers as exemplary forms.

4

THE DISORDERS OF PHILOSOPHY IN THE MIDDLE AGES

After the first flowering of philosophy in Greece in the fifth and fourth centuries B.C., there is a long period of sterility and stagnation. This is not to say that the fifteen hundred years from the end of the fourth century B.C. to the eleventh century of the Christian era are totally devoid of substantive contributions to philosophical thought. The Stoics, Epicureans, and Neoplatonists of the Hellenistic period add to the stock of philosophical theories and arguments, as do some of the early fathers of the church, especially Saint Augustine. However, looking at what happened in procedural terms, we find no development of the philosophical enterprise as such, no refinement of method, no clarification of purpose, no sharpening of boundary lines, no clearer definition of philosophical objectives.

From the perspective of this survey of philosophy's history—looking for self-understanding on the part of philosophy—the long period that follows Plato and Aristotle adds little or nothing. If anything, there is a loss of energy and clarity. Philosophy is done in a lower key and without the conscious effort at self-examination—the effort to philosophize about philosophy itself—that distinguishes the work of Plato and Aristotle.

Beginning in the middle or at the end of the eleventh century, and running to the end of the thirteenth or the middle of the fourteenth century, there is another brief period in which philosophy takes new steps forward, especially in the direction of ordering itself in relation to religion and theology. Unhappily, these gains also involve new disorders. Let us look first at the positive side of the picture.

We need not judge the validity of Christianity's claim to possess, in the Old and New Testaments, the revealed word of God in order to see how the theological effort to understand revealed truth—the dogmas of the Christian faith—not only stimulated philosophical thought, but also relieved it of a burden.

I shall refer to philosophical thought that is stimulated and enlightened by the exigencies and intellectual demands of Christian faith as Christian philosophizing. The faithful refer, instead, to Christian philosophy and mean, by that term, philosophical thought carried on in the light of faith and elevated or rectified thereby.

In order not to beg the question about the validity of this conception of a Christianized philosophy, inwardly transformed by the admixture of faith with reason, I shall use the phrase "Christian philosophizing" to call attention to the fact that something happened to philosophy when it became involved in the effort to construct a rational system of dogmatic theology in order to explain, so far as that is possible, the articles of Christian faith.

What happened was an extension of the scope of philosophical inquiry by the introduction of new questions—questions that did not occur to Plato and Aristotle, and probably could not have been formulated by them in the terms or with the precision to be found in Christian philosophizing. The most obvious example of this is the whole discussion of the freedom of the will, occasioned by the need to assess man's responsibility for sin, both original and acquired, and complicated by the doctrines of divine grace, foreknowledge, and predestination.

Though Saint Augustine and later mediaeval thinkers find much to draw upon in the writings of Plato and Aristotle with regard to other philosophical problems, they develop their elaborate doctrine of free will almost from scratch. Plato and Aristotle appear to take man's freedom of choice as an obvious fact of experience; they offer no analysis or defense of free will; it was not for them a problem, full of thorny issues, as it was for Christian philosophizing.

Another example involves the contrast between the treatment of time and eternity and the approach to the problem of the world's having or not having a beginning, as these things are discussed in Plato's *Timaeus* or Aristotle's *Physics,* Book VIII, and as they are expounded in the theological doctrine of the world's creation by God. While the last is strictly theological, ultimately based on the opening words of Genesis, it influences the philosophizing that is done within the framework or in the context of dogmatic theology. It leads Christian philosophizing to raise questions about the real distinction between essence and existence, about the difference between time and eternity, and about the causation of being or existence as compared with the causation of becoming, change, or motion. These questions do not appear in the corpus of Greek thought.

Still another example involves the refinement in later Christian philosophizing of the Aristotelian conception of substance and accident, essence and existence, matter and form, occasioned by the difficulties encountered in the theological employment of these conceptions to deal with the three great mysteries of the Christian faith—the mystery of the Trinity, the mystery of the Incarnation, and the mystery of the Eucharist.

Greek philosophers could not draw a sharp line between the domains of philosophy and religion. They could not separate questions that were answerable in the light of reason and experience from questions that were answerable only in the light of faith. In consequence, philosophy unwittingly assumed tasks it was not competent to discharge.

That burden persisted in the first phase of Christian philosophizing, during which men engaged in the fruitless effort to demonstrate the dogmas of the Christian faith as if they were philosophical conclusions. Instead of saying that the burden persisted, I should perhaps have said that it grew heavier and that the resulting distraction of philosophy from its own proper tasks became aggravated.

In addition, the excesses of rationalism on the part of philosophers such as Peter Abelard, who tried to bite off religious matters that they could not chew, generated a reaction on the part of theologians in the opposite direction. Abelard's trying to prove the Trinity is an example of his extreme rationalism.

This resulted in the excess known as fideism, which, instead of telling philosophers to mind their own business, told them that they really had no business of their own to mind— that philosophy had no autonomy as a mode of inquiry, that all important questions were answered by faith, and that all others represented idle curiosity and the vanity of worldly learning.

These opposite excesses, together with their cause—the inappropriate burden that philosophy was still carrying on its back—provoked the effort, in the second phase of Christian philosophizing, to define the spheres of faith and reason and to straighten out the tangled involvement of philosophy with religion.

The work of Thomas Aquinas culminates this effort. Being both a philosopher and a dogmatic theologian, he carefully drew the line that both related philosophy to theology and also separated their domains.

The achievement of Aquinas, in thus relieving philosophy

of the burden—the undue tasks and the distractions—of involvement in religious matters, deserves to rank with the contributions made by Plato and Aristotle to the formation and constitution of the philosophical enterprise.

Before I turn to the negative side of the picture, I must mention one other procedural gain that is made in the later Middle Ages. The universities of the thirteenth century, especially the faculties of Paris and Oxford, instituted public disputations of both philosophical and theological questions. In the *Disputed Questions* and *Quodlibetal Questions* of Aquinas, we have a one-sided record of debates in which he was himself involved, but that record nevertheless reveals a procedure in which philosophers confronted one another, joined issues, and entered into debate.

Problems are taken up in piecemeal fashion; questions are attacked one by one; objections are raised and answered. We have here, then, in these mediaeval disputations, a good procedural model for the conduct of philosophy as a public enterprise. The spirit of this procedure persists in somewhat altered form as late as the seventeenth century, in the philosophical correspondence in which both Leibniz and Spinoza engaged with critics or adversaries, and in the seven sets of objections and replies which Descartes appended to his *Meditations on First Philosophy*.

Some of the things that plagued philosophy in antiquity continued to plague it in the Middle Ages. Though not caused by philosophy's relationship to theology, they were aggravated by it. I have two manifestations of this in mind.

One is the persistence of the illusion about *epistēmē*. This was aggravated by philosophy's involvement with dogmatic theology. The latter, rightly or wrongly, made claims to certitude and finality, which had the effect of intensifying philosophy's quest for a kind of perfection in knowledge that it could never attain.

If dogmas and dogmatism are proper anywhere, it is in the theological doctrines that claim to have their foundation in the revealed word of God. While philosophy, strictly speaking, could not claim to have any dogmas or dogmatic foundations, it tried to rival theology with a certitude and finality of its own by giving its principles and conclusions the high status of knowledge in the form of *nous* and *epistēmē*.

The other manifestation is the persistence of philosophical efforts to solve, *without investigation,* problems that belong to investigative science. This, too, was aggravated by philosophy's involvement with dogmatic theology, which imbued philosophy with an undue confidence in its powers.

It should be noted here that the well-deserved respect accorded Aristotle during the later Middle Ages often turned into undue reverence and misplaced piety, in consequence of which many of the scientific errors committed by Aristotle acquired the status of unquestionable philosophical truths. When they were questioned by scientific investigators at the end of the Middle Ages, they were defended by specious philosophical reasoning that brought philosophy itself into disrepute.

Though Aquinas tried to convert theology from an absolute monarch into a constitutional ruler and to transform philosophy from a menial into a free and loyal subject, he nevertheless left the two in a hierarchical relationship of superior and inferior. And though Aquinas also tried to relieve philosophy of the questions that are answerable only by faith, he left to philosophy a number of theological questions, about God and the human soul, the answers to which he called "preambles to faith."

This helps us to understand how it came about that, at the end of the Middle Ages, when such secular philosophers as Descartes, Leibniz, and Spinoza emancipated themselves from dogmatic theology, they still retained, in their role as metaphysicians, an absorbing predilection for theological

All such questions, as I pointed out earlier, take precedence over second-order questions of the sort concerned with how we can know the answers to first-order questions.[6] A sound approach to the examination of knowledge should acknowledge the existence of some knowledge to be examined. *Knowing what can be known* is prior to asking *how we know what we know.*

Using the word "epistemology" for the theory of knowledge—especially for inquiries concerning the "origin, certainty, and extent" of our knowledge—I have two things to say about this part of the philosophical enterprise.

First, it should be reflexive; that is, it should examine the knowledge that we do have; it should be a knowing about our knowing.

Second, being reflexive, epistemology should be posterior to metaphysics, the philosophy of nature, ethics, and political theory—these and all other branches of first-order philosophical knowledge; in other words, our knowing what can be known should take precedence over our knowing about our knowing.

Both of these procedural points were violated in the critical movement that began with Locke and ran to Kant. Epistemology became "first philosophy," taking precedence over all other branches of philosophical inquiry; and, with Kant, it became the basis for "prolegomena to any future metaphysic."

Epistemology more and more tended to swallow up the whole philosophical enterprise. It is this retreat from the known world and our knowledge of it to the world of the knower and his efforts to know which prepared the way for

---

[6] See Chapter 3, *supra,* for the distinction between first- and second-order questions. First-order questions occur in the first two dimensions of philosophy, where we find knowledge about reality, both descriptive and prescriptive. Second-order questions occur in the third and fourth dimensions of philosophy, where we find philosophical analysis and the understanding of ideas and subject matters. Recent linguistic and analytical philosophy is another type of second-order discipline.

the later total retreat of philosophy (in our own century) to the plane of second-order questions, relinquishing entirely any claim to have a respectable method for carrying on first-order inquiries.

I think it is apt, and not too harsh, to call this first unfortunate result of the critical reaction to dogmatic systems "suicidal epistemologizing." Epistemology, fashioned by philosophers as a scalpel to cut away the cancer of dogmatism, was turned into a dagger and plunged into philosophy's vitals.

The second unfortunate result can, with equally good reason, be called "suicidal psychologizing." Like the first, it is also a retreat from reality. Where the first is a retreat from the reality of the knowledge that we actually do have, the second is a retreat from the reality of the world to be known. Modern idealism begins with Kant. It is the worst of the modern errors in philosophy.

What I mean by "suicidal psychologizing" is sometimes less picturesquely described as "the way of ideas," fathered by Descartes, but given its most unfortunate effects by the so-called British empiricists—Locke, Berkeley, and Hume—who made the psychologizing of common experience the whole of philosophy and substituted that for the use of common experience as a test of the soundness of philosophical theories or conclusions about the experienced world. The psychologizing of common experience deserves to be called suicidal; for, in effect, it cuts away the very ground on which the philosopher stands. It makes experience subjective, rather than objective.

I need not dwell here on the far-reaching consequences of this fundamental substantive error—the subjectivism and the solipsism that resulted from proceeding in this way, together with all the skeptical excesses that it led to, and the epistemological puzzles and paradoxes that confronted those who tried to hold onto the most obvious features of our experience after they had been psychologized into myths or illusions.

Starting from Locke's fundamental error and carrying it to all its logical conclusions, later philosophers—first Berkeley and Hume, then the phenomenalists and logical empiricists of the twentieth century—reached results that they or others had enough common sense to recognize as absurd; but though many have deplored the resulting puzzles and paradoxes, no one seems to have recognized that the only remedy for the effects thus produced lies in removing the cause, by correcting Locke's original error, the error of treating ideas as *that which* we apprehend instead of *that by which*. It is this error that makes our common experience subjective rather than objective—introspectively observable, which it is not.

I turn now to the second major disorder of philosophy in modern times—the emulation of science and mathematics. This begins in the seventeenth century. It can be discerned in Francis Bacon and Thomas Hobbes, as well as in Descartes, Spinoza, and Leibniz. Beginning then, it runs through the following centuries right down to the present day.

The philosophers of the seventeenth century, misled by their addiction to *epistēmē*, looked upon mathematics as the most perfect achievement of knowledge, and tried to "perfect" philosophy by mathematicizing it. This was done in different ways by Descartes, Spinoza, and Leibniz, but the effect upon philosophy was the same—the frustration of trying to achieve a precision of terminology and a rigor of demonstration that are appropriate in mathematics, but inappropriate in philosophy as an attempt to answer first-order questions about reality—about that which is and happens in the world or about what ought to be done and sought.

The fact that science can be mathematicized to a certain extent—the achievements of mathematical physics in particular—accentuated the mistake on the part of those who failed to see that the application of mathematics to physics depends on the special data of measurement, which have no analogue in the noninvestigative enterprise of philosophy.

This mistaken emulation of mathematics and the consequent effort to mathematicize philosophy reappear with unusual force in the twentieth century: in the "logical atomism" of Bertrand Russell, and in all the attempts to treat the language of mathematics as a modern language, to be imitated in philosophical discourse.

The effort to give philosophical discovery the simplicity of mathematical symbolism and the univocity of mathematical terms, and the effort to give philosophical formulations the "analyticity" of mathematical statements, put philosophy into a straitjacket from which it has only recently broken loose by a series of almost self-destructive convulsions.

Beginning also in the seventeenth century, philosophers began to be awed by the achievements of science and became more and more openly envious of certain features of science—the kind of progress that science makes, the kind of usefulness that it has, the kind of agreements and decisions that it can reach, and the kind of assent it wins from an ever-widening public because its theories and conclusions can be tested empirically.

Not recognizing that all these things can be achieved by philosophy in its own characteristic way, but only if it tries to achieve them in a manner appropriate to its own character as a noninvestigative discipline, philosophers over the last three hundred years have been suffering from an unwarranted sense of inferiority to science.

This sense of inferiority has, in turn, two further results. It has driven some philosophers to make all sorts of mistaken efforts to imitate science. It has led others, such as the logical positivists in our own century, to turn the whole domain of first-order inquiry over to science and to restrict philosophy

problems, as witness Descartes's *Meditations*, Leibniz's *Theodicy* and *Discourse on Metaphysics*, and Spinoza's *Ethics*.[5]

In the later Middle Ages, influenced by the conception of philosophy as a body of knowledge having the character of *epistēmē*, which philosophy's association with dogmatic theology intensified, philosophers, in dealing with the questions relegated to philosophical theology, tried to give their reasoning a demonstrative and rigorous appearance that it could not actually possess.

Thinking that they succeeded, they often went further and took over into philosophical theology matters with which reason, apart from faith, was even less competent to deal. They undid the good work of Aquinas by extending the bounds of philosophical theology to include much more than the few simple preambles to faith that he had placed on the philosophical side of the line that he drew to divide its domain from that of dogmatic theology.

This overexpanded philosophical theology—or, in some cases, religious apologetics—not only set much of subsequent Scholastic philosophy off on a wild-goose chase, it also helped to get modern philosophy off to a bad start. I have in mind the work of the three great philosophers of the seventeenth century, to whom I have already referred: Descartes, Leibniz, and Spinoza.

They were brought up and educated in a tradition of metaphysics and theology that was a heritage from the later Middle Ages and the decadent Scholasticism of the fifteenth and sixteenth centuries. Though two of them were Christians, none was a Christian philosopher in the sense of accepting the guidance of faith through the subordination of

[5] When one examines the content, language, and style of argument of these works, there is good reason to say that they represent the end of the Middle Ages as well as the beginning of modern times.

philosophy to dogmatic theology. On the contrary, they represent the revolt of philosophy from theology.

Readers must carefully examine Descartes's *Principles of Philosophy,* Spinoza's *Ethics,* and Leibniz's *Monadology* and *Discourse on Metaphysics* to see for themselves the style and manner of philosophizing, which I call system building. They will then, I hope, readily understand why I use that term in a wholly derogatory sense, especially if they bear in mind my central contention that philosophy, as a mode of inquiry, aims at knowledge in the form of testable *doxa,* not unquestionable *epistēmē.* They will realize that system building defeats or violates the procedures proper to philosophy, especially its being conducted as a public enterprise in which common questions are faced, issues are joined, and disputes can be adjudicated.

The philosophical system which is so private and special that it came to be called Cartesian, or Spinozist, or Leibnizian assumes the character of a great painting or poem, an individual artistic achievement calling for rejection or acceptance as an inviolable whole. There are, of course, Platonic, Aristotelian, Augustinian, and Thomistic doctrines in philosophy, but there is no system of Platonic, Aristotelian, or Augustinian philosophy in any comparable sense of that term.

There is some accuracy in speaking of a Thomistic system, but this should always be understood as referring to the system of theology which Aquinas presented in his *Summa Theologica,* not to a system of philosophical thought, for none can be found in or extracted from his writings.

We have here one clue to what is wrong with system building in philosophy, as well as an explanation of how it arose. Since dogmatic theology rests on the dogmas of religious faith, a system of dogmatic theology can be properly constructed by an orderly exposition and defense of these dogmas. It is the order and relationship of the dogmas, with which sacred theology begins, that give the dogmatic exposition of theology its systematic character. Clearly, I mean more here by "systematic" than thinking in an orderly and coherent way. I mean a monolithic structure, rising from a firm foundation in unchallengeable premises, such as dogmas are.

Even though they reacted against the *Summa Theologica* of Aquinas and other theological systems, the thinkers of the seventeenth century were greatly influenced by the model of system structure it offered. They were also influenced by another model of system structure—that of Euclid's *Elements*—which was as inappropriate as the theological model for philosophers to try to imitate. Yet this is precisely what Descartes, Spinoza, and Leibniz tried to do, each in his own way.

Each laid down a few "unchallengeable" premises from which he thought he could erect, by the deductive elaboration of their consequences, the whole vast structure of his thought. Each proceeded in an ostensibly deductive manner to "demonstrate" conclusions that, for him, had the certitude and finality of *epistēmē*.

Thus there came into being, for the first time in the history of philosophy, individual systems of thought, an event that caused drastic reactions and consequences in the centuries to follow. There are systems in mathematics, but there should be none in philosophy if philosophy is *doxa*, not *epistēmē*.

5

THE VICISSITUDES OF PHILOSOPHY IN MODERN TIMES

In each of the two historical epochs that we have so far surveyed—antiquity and the Middle Ages—we have found both positive and negative features. I have called the latter the misfortunes or disorders that philosophy has suffered; and the former, the good starts or gains that it has made in understanding its tasks and acquiring sound procedures for accomplishing them.

The modern period, like the ancient and the mediaeval, has its positive as well as its negative features—its turns for the better as well as its misfortunes and disorders. In telling the story of philosophy in modern times, I am going to reverse the order and postpone a consideration of philosophy's gains until I have described what I regard as the four major misfortunes or disorders that it has suffered since the seventeenth century.

The first of these misfortunes occurred in the context of an otherwise sound critical reaction to the dogmatism and pretentiousness of the philosophical systems of the seventeenth century. The critical movement in philosophy, from Locke to Kant, looked askance at these systems and challenged their unwarranted claims to be able to demonstrate and to know with certitude. It questioned as well their competence to deal with matters (both theological and scientific) beyond the proper scope of philosophical inquiry.

In both of the respects just indicated, this critical reaction was sound, and it might have been wholly on the side of gain if it had insisted, positively, on the substitution of *doxa* for *epistēmē* as the standard or grade of knowledge at which philosophy should aim. That by itself would have dealt a death blow to system building and provided an effective antitoxin against any future recurrence of the disease.

Unfortunately, the critical reaction to the systems of the seventeenth century took another course and resulted in two serious disorders. To explain the first of these, it is necessary to recall that, in the ancient and mediaeval worlds, metaphysics was called *philosophia prima*, or "first philosophy." Let me now extend the meaning of "first philosophy" to include all first-order inquiries, not only speculative questions about that which is and happens in the world but also normative questions about what ought to be done and sought.

All such questions, as I pointed out earlier, take precedence over second-order questions of the sort concerned with how we can know the answers to first-order questions.[6] A sound approach to the examination of knowledge should acknowledge the existence of some knowledge to be examined. *Knowing what can be known* is prior to asking *how we know what we know.*

Using the word "epistemology" for the theory of knowledge—especially for inquiries concerning the "origin, certainty, and extent" of our knowledge—I have two things to say about this part of the philosophical enterprise.

First, it should be reflexive; that is, it should examine the knowledge that we do have; it should be a knowing about our knowing.

Second, being reflexive, epistemology should be posterior to metaphysics, the philosophy of nature, ethics, and political theory—these and all other branches of first-order philosophical knowledge; in other words, our knowing what can be known should take precedence over our knowing about our knowing.

Both of these procedural points were violated in the critical movement that began with Locke and ran to Kant. Epistemology became "first philosophy," taking precedence over all other branches of philosophical inquiry; and, with Kant, it became the basis for "prolegomena to any future metaphysic."

Epistemology more and more tended to swallow up the whole philosophical enterprise. It is this retreat from the known world and our knowledge of it to the world of the knower and his efforts to know which prepared the way for

[6] See Chapter 3, *supra,* for the distinction between first- and second-order questions. First-order questions occur in the first two dimensions of philosophy, where we find knowledge about reality, both descriptive and prescriptive. Second-order questions occur in the third and fourth dimensions of philosophy, where we find philosophical analysis and the understanding of ideas and subject matters. Recent linguistic and analytical philosophy is another type of second-order discipline.

the later total retreat of philosophy (in our own century) to the plane of second-order questions, relinquishing entirely any claim to have a respectable method for carrying on first-order inquiries.

I think it is apt, and not too harsh, to call this first unfortunate result of the critical reaction to dogmatic systems "suicidal epistemologizing." Epistemology, fashioned by philosophers as a scalpel to cut away the cancer of dogmatism, was turned into a dagger and plunged into philosophy's vitals.

The second unfortunate result can, with equally good reason, be called "suicidal psychologizing." Like the first, it is also a retreat from reality. Where the first is a retreat from the reality of the knowledge that we actually do have, the second is a retreat from the reality of the world to be known. Modern idealism begins with Kant. It is the worst of the modern errors in philosophy.

What I mean by "suicidal psychologizing" is sometimes less picturesquely described as "the way of ideas," fathered by Descartes, but given its most unfortunate effects by the so-called British empiricists—Locke, Berkeley, and Hume—who made the psychologizing of common experience the whole of philosophy and substituted that for the use of common experience as a test of the soundness of philosophical theories or conclusions about the experienced world. The psychologizing of common experience deserves to be called suicidal; for, in effect, it cuts away the very ground on which the philosopher stands. It makes experience subjective, rather than objective.

I need not dwell here on the far-reaching consequences of this fundamental substantive error—the subjectivism and the solipsism that resulted from proceeding in this way, together with all the skeptical excesses that it led to, and the epistemological puzzles and paradoxes that confronted those who tried to hold onto the most obvious features of our experience after they had been psychologized into myths or illusions.

Starting from Locke's fundamental error and carrying it to all its logical conclusions, later philosophers—first Berkeley and Hume, then the phenomenalists and logical empiricists of the twentieth century—reached results that they or others had enough common sense to recognize as absurd; but though many have deplored the resulting puzzles and paradoxes, no one seems to have recognized that the only remedy for the effects thus produced lies in removing the cause, by correcting Locke's original error, the error of treating ideas as *that which* we apprehend instead of *that by which*. It is this error that makes our common experience subjective rather than objective—introspectively observable, which it is not.

I turn now to the second major disorder of philosophy in modern times—the emulation of science and mathematics. This begins in the seventeenth century. It can be discerned in Francis Bacon and Thomas Hobbes, as well as in Descartes, Spinoza, and Leibniz. Beginning then, it runs through the following centuries right down to the present day.

The philosophers of the seventeenth century, misled by their addiction to *epistēmē*, looked upon mathematics as the most perfect achievement of knowledge, and tried to "perfect" philosophy by mathematicizing it. This was done in different ways by Descartes, Spinoza, and Leibniz, but the effect upon philosophy was the same—the frustration of trying to achieve a precision of terminology and a rigor of demonstration that are appropriate in mathematics, but inappropriate in philosophy as an attempt to answer first-order questions about reality—about that which is and happens in the world or about what ought to be done and sought.

The fact that science can be mathematicized to a certain extent—the achievements of mathematical physics in particular—accentuated the mistake on the part of those who failed

250 EPILOGUE *Philosophy's Past, Present, and Future*

to see that the application of mathematics to physics depends on the special data of measurement, which have no analogue in the noninvestigative enterprise of philosophy.

This mistaken emulation of mathematics and the consequent effort to mathematicize philosophy reappear with unusual force in the twentieth century: in the "logical atomism" of Bertrand Russell, and in all the attempts to treat the language of mathematics as a modern language, to be imitated in philosophical discourse.

The effort to give philosophical discovery the simplicity of mathematical symbolism and the univocity of mathematical terms, and the effort to give philosophical formulations the "analyticity" of mathematical statements, put philosophy into a straitjacket from which it has only recently broken loose by a series of almost self-destructive convulsions.

Beginning also in the seventeenth century, philosophers began to be awed by the achievements of science and became more and more openly envious of certain features of science—the kind of progress that science makes, the kind of usefulness that it has, the kind of agreements and decisions that it can reach, and the kind of assent it wins from an ever-widening public because its theories and conclusions can be tested empirically.

Not recognizing that all these things can be achieved by philosophy in its own characteristic way, but only if it tries to achieve them in a manner appropriate to its own character as a noninvestigative discipline, philosophers over the last three hundred years have been suffering from an unwarranted sense of inferiority to science.

This sense of inferiority has, in turn, two further results. It has driven some philosophers to make all sorts of mistaken efforts to imitate science. It has led others, such as the logical positivists in our own century, to turn the whole domain of first-order inquiry over to science and to restrict philosophy to second-order questions, where it does not have to compete with science.

Either result is unfortunate. Philosophy should neither ape science as a first-order discipline (in view of their basic differences in method) nor be the second-order handmaiden of science conceived as the primary first-order discipline (in view of philosophy's rightful claim to its own first-order questions and its superiority to science in rendering the world intelligible).

The third major misfortune suffered by philosophy in modern times occurs by way of a reaction to a reaction. I am referring here to the counterreactionary restoration of philosophical systems in post-Kantian thought—in Georg Friedrich Hegel, Arthur Schopenhauer, and Johann Gottlieb Fichte on the Continent, and in such British Hegelians as F. H. Bradley, Bernard Bosanquet, Edward Caird, and J.M.E. McTaggart, and in American Hegelians such as Josiah Royce.

The critical reaction to the philosophical systems of the seventeenth century reached its climax and, in a sense, spent itself in the Kantian critiques. Just as that critical reaction as a whole was justified by the dogmatic excesses of the seventeenth century, so the post-Kantian counterreaction was justified by the excesses and mistakes of the critical movement from Locke to Kant—the epistemologizing and psychologizing tendencies described earlier.

However, just as the dogmatic excesses of the seventeenth century could have been corrected without foisting these new misfortunes upon philosophy, so the psychologizing and epistemologizing excesses of the critical movement could have been corrected without reinstating the very thing—the imposture of system building—that the critical movement tried to get rid of.

That, unfortunately, is not the way things happened. Instead, what I shall call the "Hegelian misfortune" befell philosophy.[7] What we have here is the evil of system building carried to its furthest possible extreme—an extreme to which, it must in all fairness be said, Hegel's more commonsense British followers did not go.

The Hegelian system is much more dogmatic, rationalistic, and out of touch with common experience than the Cartesian, Leibnizian, and Spinozist systems of the seventeenth century.

In addition, a fault intrinsic to the earlier systems becomes much more exacerbated in the Hegelian system. It offers those who come to it no alternatives except wholesale acceptance or rejection. It constitutes a world of its own and has no commerce or conversation with anything outside itself.

The conflict of systems of this sort (for example, that of Hegel and that of Schopenhauer) is totally beyond adjudication: each, like a sovereign state, acknowledges no superior jurisdiction and no impartial arbiter.

The pluralization of systems in the nineteenth century, each a personal worldview of great imaginative power and poetic scope, took philosophy further in the wrong direction than it had ever gone before—further away from the tendencies it had manifested in earlier epochs, tendencies to acquire the character of a cooperative venture and a public enterprise.

The final misfortune of modern philosophy arose, as preceding ones did, by way of reaction to an existing state of affairs. This fourth and last disorder consists in three mistaken directions taken by twentieth-century thought, having

[7] I think this appellation is justified by the fact that Hegel is the most powerful and influential of the nineteenth-century system builders, as well as the focus of all the twentieth-century reactions to his type of philosophizing. See, for example, Karl Popper's now famous diatribe against Hegel, with the spirit of which I fully agree: *The Open Society and Its Enemies* (Princeton, N.J.: Princeton University Press, 1950), Chapter 12, especially pp. 252–73; and see also Section 17 of the Addendum (1966).

one central animus in common—namely, that they all spring from a deep revulsion to the Hegelian misfortune.

There is, first of all, the existentialist reaction to Hegel and all forms of Hegelianism. I mention this first because, while it departs from Hegel in substance, it embodies two of the worst features of the Hegelian misfortune. The existentialist philosophers—Søren Kierkegaard, Martin Heidegger, Karl Jaspers, Jean-Paul Sartre, Maurice Merleau-Ponty, and Gabriel Marcel—all produce highly personal worldviews of their own, systems to be accepted or rejected as wholes, even if they are not rationalistically constructed, as Hegel's is.

The other two reactions are alike in that they both move away from Hegel in procedure as well as in substance. Both, in despair about philosophy as first-order knowledge served up in the Hegelian manner, urge philosophy to retreat to the sanity and safety of an exclusively second-order discipline.

One of these reactions to Hegel is the retreat conducted by the positivists, Viennese, British, and American. When the members of the Vienna Circle referred to "metaphysics" and attacked it as an abomination that must be forever extirpated from the philosophical enterprise, they had Hegel, and only Hegel, in mind.

The other reaction is not to Hegel himself as much as to British Hegelianism. It is the retreat conducted by the British analytic and linguistic philosophers and their American followers.

The end result of both retreats is very much the same: philosophy is relegated to the plane of a second-order discipline, that is, analytical and linguistic philosophy. However, there is this difference between them: where the positivists were content to have philosophy serve as handmaiden to science in performing second-order functions of linguistic and logical clarification or commentary, the analysts and linguists took on other second-order tasks, among them the analysis of commonsense opinions as expressed in everyday speech, and the attempt to cure the puzzles and paradoxes that are of modern philosophy's own making, by virtue of its own epistemologizing and psychologizing tendencies.

So far I have had nothing good to say about the career of philosophy in modern times. However, just as in treating the auspicious beginning that philosophy enjoyed in Greek antiquity I also pointed out that its first epoch was attended by serious misfortunes, so now, in concluding an account of philosophy in modern times, I am going to point out two auspicious developments that relieve this long tale of disorders and misfortunes. More than that, they point, I believe, to the dawn of a new day.

The first of these is, perhaps, the more important. It is the successive separation of all the positive sciences, both natural and social, from the parent stem of philosophy.

It is sometimes said that philosophy is now bankrupt because it has now fully performed its historic function of giving birth to the particular positive sciences, from astronomy and physics to psychology and sociology. If it were true that philosophy's only role in human culture is that of being the parent stem from which the particular sciences break off to lead lives of their own, then philosophy might very well be considered bankrupt—barren, dried up, finished. That, I hope I have shown, is not true.

The central fact of importance here is that only in modern times have the natural sciences gradually separated themselves from what in the seventeenth century was still called natural philosophy. Similarly, in the eighteenth and nineteenth centuries, the behavioral sciences gradually separated themselves from what was once called moral philosophy.

With these successive secessions, the scientific enterprise

as a whole finally became clearly and plainly established as an autonomous branch of human knowledge and a distinct mode of inquiry. At last, after twenty-five centuries, it becomes possible to draw a sharp line between the domains of science and philosophy; and philosophy is freed of the burden that, for lack of clarity on this point, it carried so long— the burden of treating as philosophical questions that belong to science and are outside philosophy's competence.

The second gain that has been made in modern times, almost as important as the first, is in one way only the restoration of an earlier condition beneficial to philosophy.

What I have in mind here is the contribution to the development of philosophy that has been made in our own century by the British analysts and linguistic philosophers. Their retreat to the plane of second-order questions has been accompanied by a way of doing philosophical work that is the very antithesis of personal system building, not only of the Hegelian type but of the Cartesian or Spinozist type as well.

It involves the tackling of philosophical problems, question by question; it involves cooperation among men working on the same problems; it involves the policing of their work by acknowledged standards or tests; it involves the adjudication of disputes and the settling of differences. Though this can be viewed as a return to the conception of philosophy as a cooperative enterprise, first enunciated by Aristotle, and also as a return to the spirit of the public disputations in the Middle Ages, it marks a great advance in modern times.

In spite of all the regrettable vicissitudes through which philosophy has gone in modern times, the two gains that I have just described would, if sustained and combined with the advances in the right direction made in earlier epochs, promise philosophy a future much brighter than its past.

6

PHILOSOPHY'S FUTURE

There is little point in asking whether philosophy has a future, for that question hardly admits of a negative answer. The probability is great that in some sense there will always be philosophy—in the family of disciplines, in our education, in our culture.

Nor should we ask whether philosophy *will have* a future brighter than its past. That calls for a prediction that is too hazardous to make. Nothing that has been said in this book furnishes us with grounds for defending an optimistic prediction about philosophy's future. On the contrary, what we have seen of philosophy's past may lead us to think that the opposite prediction about its future is a more likely one.

This leaves the question to which I think an answer can be given with some confidence: *Can* philosophy have a future brighter than its past? The possibility of its having such a future can be argued with some assurance. In light of philosophy's past, as recounted in the preceding pages, I can indicate why I think that philosophy *can have* a brighter future.

I shall first list the misfortunes or disorders that philosophy has suffered in the past, which it should be possible to eliminate from its future. I shall then list the good starts, gains, or advances that philosophy has made, which it should be possible to preserve, consolidate, and enhance.

(i) *The negative features of philosophy's past which can be eliminated from its future:*

1. The illusion of *epistēmē*
2. Dogmatic systems and personal system building
3. Carrying a burden of problems beyond its competence, resulting from a lack of sharp distinction of the domain of philosophy from the domain of science, on the one hand, and from the domain of religion and dogmatic theology, on the other

4. The emulation of science and mathematics in respects quite inappropriate to the conduct of the philosophical enterprise

5. Philosophy's assumption of quasi-religious status by offering itself as a way of life

6. The relinquishment of first-order inquiries to science and the retreat to second-order questions exclusively

7. Suicidal epistemologizing with all its consequences

8. The psychologizing of experience

(ii) *The positive features of philosophy's past which can be preserved, consolidated, and enhanced:*

1. Plato's and Aristotle's exploration of first-order questions, both speculative and practical. (This has been enhanced by the addition of questions posed and explored by philosophers in subsequent centuries.)

2. Aristotle's first approximation to philosophy's distinctive method, which involves common experience as a source and as a test of philosophical theories and conclusions. (This, too, can be enhanced by our ability now to make a clearer distinction between special and common experience.)

3. The separation, in modern times, of the particular positive sciences from the parent stem of philosophy. (As a result, science as an investigative mode of inquiry is at last quite distinct from philosophy as a noninvestigative mode of inquiry, though both deal with first-order questions empirically.)

4. The equally sharp separation, first seen as a possibility in the thirteenth century, of the domain of philosophy from the domain of religion or dogmatic theology. (With the realization of that possibility, philosophy should be relieved of the burden of theological questions beyond its competence, just as the clear distinction between science and philosophy relieves it of the burden of scientific questions beyond its competence.)

If the philosophical enterprise from now on took advantage of the four things just enumerated, that would give philosophy, for the first time in its history, a clearly defined domain of its own, a distinctive method of its own, and a sense of its own proper value, unembarrassed by comparisons with science, mathematics, or religion.

This is possible in the future as never before. There are, in addition, hopeful indications that, in the years ahead, philosophy can finally be exorcised of its bewitchment by the illusion of *epistēmē*, to be replaced by a sober respect for testable *doxa* as the only grade of organized knowledge that is achievable either in philosophy or science.

I hope I may be pardoned for referring here to the program of the Institute for Philosophical Research and to the work that it has done. The further prosecution of such work and the extension of it through similar undertakings in our universities would, in my judgment, advance the clarification of philosophical discourse about is own first-order theories or conclusions, and facilitate the conduct of philosophy as a public enterprise by helping philosophers to join issue and debate disputed questions.

Briefly summarized, the work of the Institute involves (a) taking stock of the whole accumulation of philosophical opinions on a given subject, (b) treating all the relevant opinions *as if* they were contemporary efforts to solve a common problem, (c) clarifying that problem by *constructing* genuine issues about it, thus defining the agreements and disagreements that can be found in philosophical discourse about the subject in question, and (d) then *constructing*, from the recorded materials, some approximation to a rational debate of the issues, so far as that is possible.

The Institute refers to the method by which it carries out this program of second-order work in philosophy as dialectical. The work of the dialectician thus conceived is an effort to clarify philosophical discourse itself. It makes no contribution to the substance of philosophical thought, nor does it impose upon philosophical thought any critical standards whereby the truth or falsity of philosophical theories is to be judged.

Its only function, to borrow a word much in use by the analytic and linguistic philosophers, is therapeutic. However, where their therapeutic efforts are directed against the puzzles and paradoxes that arise from confusions and mistakes in the substance of philosophical thought, the dialectical effort attempts to remedy the deficiencies in philosophical thought which arise from a procedural rather than a substantive failure on the part of philosophers—their failure to conduct philosophy as a public enterprise wherein they engage collectively and cooperatively in the pursuit of truth.

I am proposing that second-order work in philosophy, of the dialectical type represented by the Institute's efforts to clarify the state of philosophical opinion about FREEDOM, LOVE, PROGRESS, HAPPINESS, JUSTICE, and the like, should be extended to cover the whole field of recorded philosophical thought, even though that is a project of gargantuan proportions.

I am, further, proposing that dialectical work of this kind should be sustained as a continuing and essential part of the whole philosophical enterprise, subsidiary, as all second-order work should be considered, to the main philosophical effort on the plane of first-order questions.

If these things were done, the main effort could be much more effectively prosecuted in the future, for it would be carried on in the light of a much better understanding than philosophers now have of the contributions, both cumulative and conflicting, that have been made to the solution of their first-order problems.

One might even hope that eventually there need be no division of labor between dialecticians working at their second-order tasks and philosophers trying to answer first-order questions. Philosophy might finally become the collective and cooperative pursuit that it should be—an enterprise in which the individual participants communicated effectively about their common problems, joined issue when their solutions were opposed, and engaged in rational debate for the sake of resolving their disagreements and reaching whatever measure of agreement is attainable in the field of debatable opinion.

I conclude with one last summary of the argument. *If* the negative features of philosophy's past are eliminated from its future, as they *can be*—and *if* the positive features that I have enumerated are preserved, consolidated, and enhanced, as they also *can be*—then it follows that philosophy *can have* a future brighter than its past.

The full realization of the possibility just indicated may require a future far beyond the present century. The twenty-five centuries of philosophy's Western past may be at the most the period of its infancy—its first uncertain steps and stumblings. The gradual achievement of maturity in the philosophical enterprise may require a much longer span than the three hundred years—from the seventeenth century to the present—during which science appears to have outgrown its infancy and to have matured.

One reason for this delayed maturity may be that philosophical problems are more difficult than scientific ones, humanly speaking, if not intellectually. To conduct philosophical discussion fruitfully requires greater discipline of the passions than is needed to carry on scientific investigation in an efficient manner.

It is easier to lift scientific research to the high plane of the near-perfect experiment than to lift philosophical discussion to the high plane of the ideal debate. In addition, the philosophical enterprise may be a much more complex form of intellectual life than the scientific endeavor is; and, like all higher organisms, therefore slower to mature.

Considering man's biological origins, we should, perhaps, be filled with admiration that human beings took less than six thousand years after they emerged from the conditions of primitive life to produce the civilization of the dialogue. Six thousand years is a short period in the span of human life on earth; and the twenty-five hundred years of the philosophical enterprise so far is shorter still.

It should not tax our imaginations, therefore, to contemplate a much longer future in which the latent possibilities for philosophy's development are realized and philosophy gradually achieves intellectual maturity.

INDEX

Abelard, Peter, 240
Abstract ideas, 39–40, 147
Action versus production, 60
Aestheticism, 80–81
Analytical and linguistic philosophy, xvii, 231
   methodology, 255
   as second-order work, xv, 14, 18–19, 49–50, 145, 247n, 253–54
Appearance, related to perception and reality, 84–98
Aquinas, Thomas, 78, 222n, 240–42
   Disputed Questions, 241
   Quodlibetal Questions, 241
   Summa Theologica, 244, 245
Aristotle, 45, 138, 242
   acknowledgment of *doxa,* 235
   confusion on mathematics, 236–37
   contributions to philosophy, 47–48, 125–26, 229, 230–32, 255, 257
   errors in, 37, 125, 126, 232, 242
   Ethics, 29, 125, 126, 233
   free will considered by, 239
   interest in *epistēmē,* 235–37
   Metaphysics, 77, 107, 230, 233
   Organon, 146
   Physics, 233, 239
   Politics, 126, 132
   Posterior Analytics, 236
   Rhetoric, 146

scientific speculations, 65, 232–33
   On the Soul, 230
   theological speculations, 233, 239
   truth defined by, 29, 83, 133
Aristotle for Everybody, 47–48
Armchair thinking, 8–9
Art, idea of, 197–98
Artificial intelligence, 35–36
Atomism, 39, 98–99, 107
Augustine, Saint, 237, 239
Autonomy
   of branches of knowledge, 7, 33
   of philosophy, xxv, 3, 7
   relative, 33
Ayer, A. J., 11

Bacon, Francis, xvi, 61, 249
Becoming
   realm defined, 120
   temporal modalities, 121
Being
   antithesis, 122
   contingent, 120–21
   inertia of, 120
   realm defined, 120
Bergson, Henri, 65
Berkeley, George, 248, 249
   idea of "notions," 39–40
   influence on philosophy, xvi
   nominalism, 26, 40, 147
Big bang theory, 37–38
Bosanquet, Bernard, 251
Bradley, F. H., 31, 251

263

"Modern Science and Ancient Wisdom," xxvi
Modes of existence, 103–4, 109–10, 113–14
Modes of inquiry, 8–9, 15–16, 51, 53–54, 225
Monadology (Leibniz), 244
Moore, G. E., 47
Moral philosophy, 29, 62, 75, 77, 104, 105, 254
 categorical imperative in, 125, 128
 dependence on metaphysics, 148
 difference from political philosophy, 133
 timelessness of, 125–26
 See also Ethics; Natural moral law
Moral virtue
 defined, 130
 self-regarding and other-regarding aspects of, 131
 unity of, 130–31

Nationalism, 141
Natural history, 15, 24
Natural moral law
 idea of, 204–5
 immutability, 140
 recognition in relation to technology, 139–40
Natural philosophy, 254
Natural rights, 134, 136, 139
 immutability, 139, 140
 recognition in relation to technology, 139–40
Nature of the Physical World, The (Eddington), 89–93, 97
Nazism, 81
Neoplatonists, 237
Newton, Isaac, xiv–xv
Nihilism, 81
Nominalism, 26, 40–41, 147
Noncontradiction principle, 32
Nous, 26, 235, 236, 242

Objective realism, 83

Objects of thought
 character of, 111–20
 defined, 110–11, 145
 intentional existence of, 110–11, 112, 113, 119, 120, 121
 mutable versus immutable, 120
 perceptually instantiated, 123
 See also Ideas (objective)
On Being and Essence (Aquinas), 78
On the Soul (Aristotle), 230
Opinion
 doxa, 6, 32*n*, 44, 224, 231, 235, 245, 246, 258
 personal, 6
Organon Aristotle), 146

Penn, William, 141
Perception, 110, 114, 146
 related to appearance and reality, 84–98
Phenomenalists, 249
Phenomenology, xvii
Philosophers
 cooperation among, 225, 255, 259–60
 debate among, 58, 241, 255, 258, 259–60
 essentialist versus anti-essentialist, 80–81
Philosophical discourse
 distinction from dialectical discourse, xxiv, 258–59
 jargon-filled, 48
Philosophical doctrines, xx–xxi, 53
 criteria of excellence, 41–42
 inconsistent, 39–41, 45
 personal system building, 244–45, 246, 252, 256
 truth in, 33–34
Philosophical physics, 77
Philosophical psychology, 34, 77, 148
Philosophical theology, 34, 77, 207, 243